The Mindful Living series

# Mindfulness at Work

Also by Oli Doyle

*Mindfulness Plain & Simple*
*Mindfulness for Life*
*Mindful Parenting*
*Mindful Relationships*

# Mindfulness
# at Work

Turn Your Job into a Gateway to Joy,

Contentment and Stress-free Living

**Oli Doyle**

This edition first published in Great Britain in 2017
by Orion
an imprint of the Orion Publishing Group Ltd
Carmelite House, 50 Victoria Embankment,
London, EC4Y ODZ
An Hachette UK Company

1 3 5 7 9 10 8 6 4 2

A CIP catalogue record for this book
is available from the British Library.

Paperback ISBN: 978 1 4091 6752 5

Printed and bound by CPI Group (UK), Ltd, Croydon, CR0 4YY

Every effort has been made to fulfil requirements with regard to
reproducing copyright material. The author and publisher will
be glad to rectify any omissions at the earliest opportunity.

MIX
Paper from
responsible sources
FSC
www.fsc.org    FSC® C104740

www.orionbooks.co.uk

To you, whoever you are, who seeks light
in the apparent darkness.

# Acknowledgements

Gratitude beyond measure to my teachers along the path: Nirgun John, Ekai Korematsu Osho, Byron Katie and Eckhart Tolle, and to all who laid the foundation for them, I can never express my thanks.

Thanks eternally to Ren, Liam, Freya and Ezra, you're all just perfectly mad and I love it. Thanks to Mum and Dad, and to Phil and Abby for all that you do, and all that you have done, it means a lot.

A humble bow to my mindfulness family all over the world, who keep in touch and share the journey with me, thank you for walking this path together.

By day, I get to practise all this with Kate, Karen, Jaz, Kris, Anne, Gabby (Gabs), Sue and Lou, and I miss practising it with Danny and Jess. You guys are the best, thank you forever.

It takes a village (almost) to write a book. Thanks to Jill and Sarah from Orion for all your help and support, none of this happens without you. Thanks to Jane from Graham Maw Christie, agent of the century and great value.

And finally, thanks to *you*, for being ready to change your world. I'm right here to help, whatever you need.

# Contents

# Introduction

For many people, work is a source of fulfilment, enjoyment, challenge and reward. It is a chance to contribute, to learn and to be a part of a team. For others, it is a drag, draining their energy as they try to stay afloat between weekends. And for most of us, work swings between stressful and enjoyable, or so it appears.

But what if work wasn't good or bad, fulfilling or menial? What if all that happened in your mind? And what if, through approaching work differently, you could find lasting happiness? That is what this book is all about. As it turns out, our happiness and our stress are not determined by what happens *out there* in the world but by what happens *in you*. If what you see happening draws you into thinking and you get lost in that world of past and future, of concepts and ideas, it will always feel stressful eventually. But if you can pull your attention back and experience the awareness, the stillness that is always there watching, even when the mind is noisy, then what happens around you will stop seeming so important. Drama will start to dissolve and you will be left to appreciate the life you have right now, instead of seeking something better in the imaginary future.

Ironically, from that place of contentment, you may well find that things change around you, that your situation improves and that life looks after you. You can still work to change the trajectory of your career, to improve your organisation and to become better at what you do, but this arises from the natural desire to be your best, not the hope for future achievement, so the energy behind it is calm, peaceful and quiet.

Work has a job to do on you, and it's not to make you happy, nor to make you rich; it is to show you the way to your true nature, and that is the role of this book also.

This is no ordinary productivity guide, nor is it a ten-step plan for less stress at work. Instead, *Mindfulness at Work* will show you how to use the challenges, the stresses and the difficulties that work stirs up in you to discover lasting peace and happiness. Because, as it turns out, happiness is not something you experience, it is who you are underneath all that thinking and problem-making.

Mindfulness is the art of stepping out of thinking and into the present moment, which allows you to discover who you are under all the mental noise. When you discover, and start to live from, the awareness that is there beneath all that mind stuff, life becomes very enjoyable indeed. Mindfulness is one way to discover that place.

Mindfulness is simple and effective and can be put into practice anywhere, so on this journey I won't use any jargon or spiritual concepts, and you will have ample opportunity to put the skills you learn into practice.

## How to read this book

*Mindfulness at Work* is designed as a six-week course, with a different theme each week, a different topic each day and a new activity to try out this way of living each day too.

You can use it that way if you wish, reading a passage each day and doing that day's activity. Alternatively, you might like to choose a day at random, or read a few days at once. My only encouragement, though, is to make sure you take the time to try the activities, which is where the words become yours, so to speak. As you read, they may make sense or not, but in the practice itself, you will be able to check what is real and true for you.

I am most happy to support you along this journey, so feel free to email me (oli@peacethroughmindfulness.com.au), check out my closed group on Facebook – Mindfulness with Oli Doyle – or track me down some other way. I love hearing from people who are on this journey too, so don't be shy.

So let's begin! Welcome to the present moment and welcome to the journey into yourself. It's the most amazing, rewarding and exciting adventure there is.

# WEEK 1

## Working in This Instant

As we begin the practical part of this journey, we will begin in the only moment there is, right here, now. As we shift our attention into this instant over the course of this week, strange things may start to occur. You may find that what used to be a problem at work no longer bothers you, that things that seemed very important aren't anymore, and that things which seemed insignificant matter much more than you imagined.

This is how mindfulness turns our world upside down. Everyday dramas lose their pull, while the leaves blowing down the street and the path of the clouds across the sky become suddenly unmissable. Welcome to the present moment.

This week we will explore how to use work to bring you into this instant, and what to do once you are there. The steps are simple indeed, but underlying them is great power. So welcome once again to the journey of a lifetime; the journey into now.

# Day 1: The Only Productive Moment

Traditionally, productivity is measured by your output over time, how many things you managed in a week, a year or a decade. Many great productivity coaches and authors will also ask you to consider how effective, how valuable the work you choose to do is, alongside the volume. But today we will narrow your productivity down to this very instant in time, for a very simple reason.

Actually, the only time you can get anything done is now, it is the moment of action. What you did, and what you will do, belong to the past and the future, which only exist as memory and as projection, as thoughts in your mind. It is pretty obvious that to do something, you must do it now. Of course, you can plan and you can reflect, and both can be useful, but when it comes to acting, it must be this instant, and missing this point causes problems for many people.

Because although what I just said is obvious, most of us live as if what we will do later is more important than fully engaging in what we are doing now, and we prioritise deciding over doing. If you have ever sat through a strategic planning day you will know what I mean. People at those events often act as if the problems discussed were already solved because there is a 'good plan'. But go to a few planning days at the same organisation and you will see that the problem is not a lack of planning, but a lack of action in the moment.

And in your own life and career you may also notice that much energy is wasted pondering what to do next or reliving what just was, reducing your capacity to be there at your best, right now. Meetings can be a classic example of this: often held without purpose, they end up as a trawl through what happened recently and a look at what we hope for next, without an emphasis on taking action *now*. This robs us of our energy and power, leaving us feeling frustrated, stuck or bored as the same issues get rehashed on rotation. Of course, planning and reflecting are fine when needed, but most humans live excessively in the past and the future (which is to say, in their heads), with little energy left over for now. Attention is a finite resource in that you can only focus on one thing at a time. If you are busy thinking about some other time and place, then chances are that you will miss what is happening here and now.

At work, this habit translates into stress and poor quality work, because you can only do something well when you pay attention to what you are doing. But more importantly, when we work in this way, we miss a great opportunity. Work can be your mindfulness practice, which means that you can use work as a way to move your attention from thinking to awareness, from mind to life as it is happening. And here is a simple exercise to try this out for yourself.

### Activity – Nowfulness at Work

In a moment, once you have read this passage, put this book down and close your eyes. Take your attention away from the stream of mind and feel your feet instead. Wriggle your toes and notice how that feels right now. Sense how warm or cool your feet are and feel them against the floor. If you have shoes or socks on, notice what this is like.

Open your eyes and stand up, feeling every movement involved in that process. Now walk across the room with intense alertness, notice every step, the feel of your feet, your breath, the movement of your legs, be present and aware of each instant.

Now imagine bringing this level of awareness to everything you do at work. Imagine if you were that attentive when you went about your daily work life. What would it be like to work with such alertness?

Pick an activity that you do each day at work. Just for today, bring this level of mindfulness to each step in the process. Feel your breath and your body, and be aware and clear as you do it. If (or when) your mind distracts you, just come back to what you are doing as soon as you notice you have drifted away.

Take stock afterwards and see how working in this way compares to your usual way of doing your job. How did it feel to be completely there as you did that task? And what would it be like to work, and live like that, anchored in the present moment?

Of course, there are times when you need to plan and reflect, and as this journey continues, we will explore ways to do those tasks mindfully too. But for now, let me ask you: how often do you really need to be thinking in order to get your job done? Your mind may say 'always', but don't be so quick to answer. Over the next few days, take note of all the things that you already know how to do, tasks in which thinking actually gets in the way of high quality work. You may be surprised at how often you would be better off with a pinch of thinking and several cups of attention, instead of the other way around.

# Day 2: Instant Purpose

As you will see as we travel this path together, there are different levels when it comes to purpose. Most people think of purpose as working towards an outcome that you have in your head beforehand, but as mindfulness students, our purpose is a little different.

The 'primary purpose' of your life (thank you Eckhart Tolle for finding that term) is to be mindful, to be alert and aware right now. So as you go about your daily work, the most important thing is whether your attention is anchored in this moment or lost in thinking.

Your 'secondary purpose' (thanks again, Eckhart) is whatever the world asks you to do on a day-to-day basis, but this is not exactly what you may think of at first. Our minds jump straight to some grand mission, or some 'meaningful' work, which may lead to fantasies about what you 'could' or 'should' be doing, but this is overcomplicating things. Right now, the world is asking you to do something, which is to read this book. In the next ten seconds, something else may call for your attention, but right this second you are reading, and that is your secondary purpose.

Personally, sometimes I forget my primary purpose and my mind dislikes my secondary purpose, or confuses it at least. Last week, I spent a whole day in a meeting that didn't seem to be going anywhere and although I had moments of presence to keep me sane, my mind became increasingly agitated as the day went on. I believed that I 'could have' been somewhere else and that my life would have been better in the office than in a long meeting. But let's rewind that a minute and pull it apart. I couldn't have gone to that meeting, nor stayed there, without the world helping to make that happen. Trains ran (which is rather unusual where I live), my legs walked, my alarm went off, my bike tyres stayed inflated. All this and a million things more made sure that I got there. In my mind's argument against what was, there was one underlying assumption: the universe made a mistake. The world messed up, it miscalculated, and now I'm stuck, and it's the fault of the meeting organiser, or whoever. Actually, my mind doesn't care whose fault it is, as long as there is someone to blame and an argument to be had, because that is what keeps it alive.

But, knowing that my mind operates this way, I don't need to believe it. When I woke up out of that stream of thinking, I realised that my secondary purpose was to be there that day, to bring something to that meeting. Whether it was obvious to me, or whether the underlying purpose never reveals itself, I was there because the world wanted me to be. And I still may not go to the next one. That's the great thing about living instant by instant: you're not committed to doing that forever, just for now.

So what about you? What in your work life are you resisting, even though the world is asking you to do it?

## Activity – Finding Resistance

Take a pen and a piece of paper in hand and finish the following sentences as quickly as you can:

*The thing I know I shouldn't have to do anymore is …*
*If life was fair, I could spend more time …*

*The person who is to blame for me being stuck in that situation is . . .*

*To be happy, I know I have to avoid . . .*

Now put your paper aside and close your eyes for a moment. Imagine that life is no more than an opportunity to learn and grow, and that you trust life to provide whatever you need for that to happen in each moment.

Picture how you might live your work life (and your whole life) if you held these two assumptions:

- My purpose is to be mindful.
- My purpose is to do whatever is in front of me right now, as well as I can.

Spend a few minutes noticing how you would approach life differently with these two assumptions in your heart.

This approach is counterintuitive, and your mind may well dismiss it outright, but allow yourself to stay curious. What would be lost if you dropped all resistance to what arises and just did your best, with as much awareness as possible?

And of course, 'do what arises' doesn't mean doing your whole job, just what is in front of you now. Each instant is a world of its own, and outside of the story of 'my job' or 'my career', you will find that work is quite simple when you just do what is asked of you right now.

At the very least, try it and see.

# Day 3: How to Relate Right Now

Relationships are a clear area of difficulty for human beings, and this comes to the forefront in our workplaces on a regular basis. Indeed, most problems at work seem to arise because of things that other humans do. Of course, problems only exist in our minds. What happens in the world is a situation, not a problem. Yet it seems as if relating with others at work creates many difficulties for us, when in fact the true cause is a little deeper.

If you watch your mind closely, you will discover that all relationship problems exist either in the past or the future. They consist of memories, replayed and dissected at length, or projections of what will happen next, or what I need to do about the problem. If you narrow your relationships down to this instant, there can never be a problem. Others may still yell, or manipulate, or ignore you, but in this instant, the only thing you can do is to work with this as well as you can. This may mean telling the person that they are being unreasonable and leaving. It may mean resigning. Or it may mean staying and pointing out the opportunities for improvement that you see.

And beyond the problems that arise, the potential for human relationships to be rich, loving and fun is immense. We are social beings, and only excessive thinking can get in the way of having a wonderful time together at work and in life.

Today I spent most of my time with people I haven't known for that long, a few years at most, a few hours at least, and if my mind had been busy thinking about the past and the future, charting the right course for me, this time together would have been stressful. A few years ago, I would have worried about what they might think of me, I would have thought about what to say and how to say it, I would have been what we call 'self-conscious'. Actually, to be self-conscious means to be mindful, to be aware of your inner world as you experience the outer. Thinking too much is more like being 'self-unconscious'. In this state, we interpret everything that is said and done, wondering what it means for 'me'. We try to work our way to the best future rather than appreciating what is here, now. And we may even inadvertently treat others poorly out of fear, greed and desire.

But today, I was free of all this. I was present, aware of what others were saying and doing, and enjoying the flow of it in this very instant. I listened with care and words came spontaneously, and they were right. We laughed, we joked, we were serious at times too, and as I walked out of the office I felt deeply connected, I felt a sense of oneness with those wonderful people. If my mind was in charge, I would have noticed their faults, limitations and contradictions, but today there were none of those. Instead, there were people doing their best, coming together to make something of this work that brought us all together.

It is easy to get along with your work colleagues if you do two things in their presence: drop your shared past and forget about the future. Of course, you might talk about a shared experience and you might make practical plans for next week, and both of these activities are fine. Dropping the past means dropping your story of who the person is, which is always based on interpreted memories. Joanne is stubborn and difficult, Andrew is cunning and sly, and when these mental labels are believed completely, you will see those people through that lens. Instead, you can stop all of that and experience that person as they are, right here and now.

This gets more challenging when someone who seems

unreasonable has power over you, like your boss, or when someone appears to be deliberately bullying you. But if you can focus your attention in on this instant and work from there, these situations (and the thoughts and feelings that arise in their aftermath) become easier to manage. You might still take action to put an end to what is happening if you can, but you can do this from a place of peace and confidence.

## Activity – Relating Right Now

When you spend time with your colleagues today, try this simple shift: be more interested in seeing them clearly, listening carefully and being present with them than you are in what your mind says.

You can start with a few mindful breaths, feeling the air come into your body and flow out again. Make the feeling of breathing the focus of your attention and allow this awareness to bring you into this moment. As you breathe, look at those around you with interest and curiosity, not to be able to label and judge them, but to experience them just as they are, right now. Look without judging, and listen carefully to what they say. Make listening your primary focus (instead of thinking about what to say next) and allow words to come naturally. When you listen closely, the right words will come at the right time.

Try interacting in this way as often as you can. There is no need to be overly quiet (although you may speak less), you can just be you, a more mindful version perhaps, but yourself nonetheless. Notice how it feels to interact in this way and see if it changes the way you view those you spend your days working alongside.

Something magical happens when you approach relationships in this way: all of a sudden everyone seems perfect just as they are. And when you have this kind of acceptance for others, they are bound to enjoy your company, and all will be well in your life. All this from just looking and listening without judgement. How simple life can be!

## Day 4: Getting Better Now

When organisations and individuals seek to improve, it's usually through a five-year plan. Set some SMART (specific, manageable, achievable, realistic, time-framed) goals, read some books on smashing those goals and find ways to measure your improvement. There's nothing wrong with this approach, as long as you understand the moment of improvement.

You see, these plans often make one false assumption: that improvement will happen sometime in the future. Remember the future? That's a thought in your head. It never comes. So if you're hoping to improve 'sometime', then there is no need to take action today, there's always tomorrow after all.

In reality, improvement either happens now or never, and it's generally not achieved by focusing on an outcome. Outcomes also exist either in the past or in the future, so setting a goal to get some particular result, though mentally satisfying, is out of alignment with reality unless you are careful.

It's possible to set goals and still be mindful, but to do this, you need to put those goals, those outcomes down as soon as you have set them. For example, at the moment, I am steadily improving my exercise regime, which last month was almost non-existent. When you take a full-time job, throw in the writing of three books in three months (as we're expecting a baby in a month's time), you have a recipe for a sedentary lifestyle it seems. Except I know when to improve.

Today is the only day I can change, and even though tomorrow seems like a much better day to do some exercise, it never seems to arrive! So I have no goal, except to improve my process, so each day, I have an aim to walk a certain distance, to do a certain number of push-ups etc. And it works. No weight-loss goals, no marathons to run, just 8km to walk today and fifty push-ups to do (and 1000 words to write). And when that gets too easy, I'll increase it. Simple.

At work, I use the same approach. When I supervise staff in my role, I aim to listen more than I talk (two ears, one mouth), to ask open questions and to reflect back what I hear. I watch for the parts of the session that don't have value and I eliminate them, so every day I get a little better.

This way of improving has some other benefits too. Because I watch myself so closely, I notice that I'm constantly short of perfection, there is always a way to improve. This is the nature of the universe, still evolving after billions of years, so of course it is the way for me too! And in this awareness, it almost feels as if I was watching someone else make those mistakes, so there's no sense of guilt or shame, just another opportunity. All this adds up to improvement without stress.

## Improving Process

Think of an outcome you would like in your work life. Choose something you can do without anyone else needing to change, like managing your time more effectively. Close your eyes and picture the things you need to practise every day to do this, like clearing your inbox every morning or reviewing your calendar when you arrive at work.

Write down three daily practices that would contribute to this outcome, for example:

1) *Clear my inbox at 9am.*
2) *Check my calendar at 9.10am.*
3) *Check my calendar again at 5pm.*

Keep your practices simple and do-able.

1) _____
2) _____
3) _____

Then, when you get to work, observe yourself as you do one of three things: do the practice, put off doing the practice or forget the practice.

If you do any or all of your three, be mindful as you do them and notice what it is like to bring them into your day. If you avoid or forget, notice what happened instead and what got in the way.

Use this process to keep working at your improvements and you will be surprised how quickly things can change with a little awareness and consistency.

Whether you do none of them or all three, bringing awareness into your day has two positive benefits. Firstly, you will learn more about yourself and your mind, and secondly, you will bring mindfulness into your work day.

For me, being mindful at work makes what I do enjoyable (except when I forget to be present) as well as challenging and rewarding. For me, this reward is the joy of fully engaging with a challenge in this moment, looking for a way to move forward and improve. This process is an end in itself, and no external results are needed to make it fulfilling, although external results usually come anyway when you increase the quality of what you do by becoming more attentive to the doing itself.

So I have seen my skills and performance consistently improve where others I know have stayed fairly stable, getting a little better or a little more tired. Some of them are more intelligent than me, better trained and more experienced, but they are lost in thought most of the time, rarely aware of their process. So while they're thinking about their next holiday, I am noticing what I do and why, I am looking for the next improvement and I am enjoying every step.

For anyone who wants peace and enjoyment at work, I highly recommend ditching your outcomes and diving headfirst into awareness of your process. You'll never look back.

## Day 5: This Conflict, This Instant

I always thought that I didn't do conflict well, but today I learned that I was wrong all along. It's not that I don't do it well, it's that I don't do it *now*.

It has been quite a week. I hit some serious speed humps

at work with a colleague I respect and a process that didn't sit well with me. This time last week I noticed some frustration in myself and some challenging thoughts bubbling away, but I ignored them. Actually, I watched them, but I didn't talk through my worries with my colleague, I let things simmer underneath until today we finally cleared the air. And I was all wrong.

As usual with conflicts, what I thought was happening wasn't, and what I believed was the right path wasn't, and I can see this clearly in hindsight. But this morning I was convinced, and some of that emotion crept into the conversation we shared and I overreacted. Luckily, my overreaction is pretty mild, so no harm was done, but it got me thinking about the path I could have taken in this and other situations to use conflict as a way to move forward now.

If I had asked a few questions and requested some time to discuss things a week ago, my last seven days would have been different and I would have better understood what was happening and why. But I brooded instead, thinking I was being kept in the dark, when in fact I never asked! Madness!

Perhaps you notice the same thing happening in *your* mind sometimes, with minor difficulties being blown out of proportion by assumptions and jumping to conclusions. It's so easy to just ask, but the mind sometimes prefers to create its own story by filling in the gaps with conspiracy theories and negative judgements.

Luckily, though, the path out of this is simple. Ask. Is what you think is happening really happening? Did the other person intend to do that? Does it mean what you think it means? I'll show you what I mean using my own example to hopefully save you from making the same mistake!

## Activity – Ask It Now

Bring to mind a drama you are experiencing at the moment or one you can remember. Recall if you can the specifics of the situation, as well as the assumptions you believed and the stories your mind created to fill in the gaps.

Write down what you were believing in that moment (or what you believe now) about the situation. Start like this:

*I believe . . .*

For example, my mind told me that I was being sidelined because they didn't trust me or value my work, so I would write:

*I believe they sidelined me because they don't trust me or value my work.*

Of course, I was wrong.

Next, write down the questions you could have asked (or could ask, if the situation is ongoing) to check if your assumptions were true. Start like this:

*I could have asked . . .*

For example, I could have asked why I wasn't being included in a particular process or decision. I could have asked, 'So you don't want me in there? Why's that?' So I would write:

*I could have asked why they asked me not to attend that meeting.*

Read back over your answers and consider the possibility of asking those questions to the people concerned. What if you just asked, rather than assuming you know what is going on in their minds? How might this change your experience and your relationship with the situation?

An ounce of curiosity saves several tonnes of regret! When I finally asked about why I hadn't been invited to that meeting, it turned out to be a simple misunderstanding. All of a sudden, the hot air fuelling the drama in my mind escaped and there was space and peace once more. My mind was almost disappointed at this, but *I* felt much better, and I was able to relate to the person I was with in a kind, compassionate way that was difficult during the internal drama.

Have a go at this yourself by applying curiosity to the assumptions that lead you down a destructive mental path. Write down the beliefs your mind holds dear and then look for ways to test their reality.

Checking the conclusions your mind has jumped to is a wonderfully simple way to take the stress out of relationships at work and in life, while also leading to a greater connection with others. This is built on openness and honesty, and every seeming conflict can become a chance to move deeper by checking your beliefs and being curious, again and again.

## Day 6: What Work Can Give You

Many people see work as a means to an end, a way to get money, recognition and social position. Others may see it as a way to contribute, gaining a sense of purpose from the positive impact their work has on the world.

But these are concepts that tend to be reliant on time, they are in the future based on the work you did in the past. You get paid next week for the work you did today and you win Citizen of the Year for what you did six months ago.

But what if work had the power to make your whole life experience more enjoyable, peaceful and complete right now? What if the experience of working could help you to connect with your true self and find inner contentment, regardless of the nature of the work? As it turns out, this is entirely possible if we make a small change in the way we see the work we do. Happiness comes from being present instead of thinking your way through life, and today we will explore how making this small change can turn work into a gateway to that peace and contentment.

Walking in the door, I notice the way the hallway lights look at this time of the morning. I hear the footsteps of my colleagues and I feel my feet walking down the hallway towards reception. I sign in, and I walk up the stairs, feeling each step and noticing the sensations in my muscles as the journey continues. Throughout this trip from the door to my desk, I feel a sense of peace and aliveness, all because I don't care about my work.

Alright, let me back up and explain this a little more, lest you think I am some sort of desk-occupying bureaucrat just waiting for their pension to kick in. I'm about as far from that as you can get. I delight in my work almost every day. I laugh, I work hard, I innovate and I do my best with every single task, and at the same time I don't care about the results.

It's not that I want to do bad work, or that I'm hard-hearted, it's just that I realised a few years ago that caring is synonymous with future. Concerning yourself with what happens next involves thinking about what may happen, deciding on the 'best' outcome and then checking reality against it. This is a stressful and ineffective way to work, and live.

On the other hand, if you use the experiences you have to bring you more fully into this instant, then that future starts to fade. This allows full concentration on what you are doing now, which guarantees your best possible work. But more importantly, you can live 'happily never after', as I like to call it: happy now, with your attention never 'after' (in the future).

Everything in your life is there to help you to discover this natural state of peace, and work is no exception. Here is a simple activity you can use to transform your daily work into a path to peace and tranquility.

## Activity – Separating the Bits

If you look at it more closely, the concept of 'my job' is a story in your mind. It's a useful story, because it helps you to know where to turn up each day, at what time, but it's a thought nonetheless. The reality of your job is what you are doing now; everything else is just a memory or a projection.

Pick a simple task you do at work each day, like checking email. When you do that task the usual way, you probably find yourself either trying to get through it and on to the next thing, or thinking about something else while you are doing it.

Today, see if you can do two things while you complete that task:

- Be completely mindful. Feel your breath and pay close attention to the task, feeling every movement and hearing every sound.

- Act as if there is nothing before or after this task. Do it with pure attention, without trying to get any particular result or get on to the next task. Act as if this moment is your whole life.

  Be practical, of course. Don't spend the entire day mindfully checking your email. You can still work at a reasonable pace, although the internal feeling of rushing may disappear, and you can still prepare for the future by responding to emails and making plans, just do it with awareness and presence.

Once you have tested this approach with some simple tasks and found that the world doesn't collapse around you, expand it to include more and more parts of your daily work. As you continue to add this level of awareness to your daily work, you will discover that doing good work is just a fringe benefit, and that the real achievement is being completely present in this very instant. The rest is just the icing on the cake.

## Day 7: What Now?

Culturally, we are mad in the way we drive ourselves forward. The combination of the cult of productivity, the Protestant work ethic and the modern penchant for busy-ness, as I like to call it, pushes us to do, do and do. Being isn't valued, because it appears to be a waste of time, which could be used to do something 'useful'.

As I watch my colleagues at work, I see this as plain as day. They sit and they stare. The screen appears captivating, as if the words, the information, the emails read and answered and deleted, held some mystical value. Watching my friend Jo is almost scary, it's as if the computer has chained her to the desk, and her face glows as if she's sitting at the feet of the oracle.

But from the other side of the room I can see clearly that Jo is trapped. She is doing low-value, low-impact work that pushes chemicals into her system because she is 'getting things done'. What did she 'get done' yesterday? Who could remember? What impact has her work had on herself or the world around her? It's hard to tell. Jo's boss loves this kind of approach, of looking busy all the time, and so Jo's work identity is all wrapped up in the idea of productivity, and the idea of doing nothing for a moment is uncomfortable. Why is this so for so many? Why is it so difficult to just stop, to be content being you, not being a productive member of the team?

In truth, your mind is afraid. Its existence only continues through movement and activity; it ceases to exist when you stop thinking. And so, your mind fears being as it looks like annihilation, it looks as if 'you' were disappearing. This sounds dramatic, but if you experience a moment or two of non-thinking, you will find that it isn't scary at all, it's just quiet and peaceful. When that chattering voice you thought was you drops away, life is amazing, but that voice fears it's own destruction, so it keeps you distracted.

I sometimes do the same to my kids when I don't want them to notice something: I just keep talking away until it's gone, filling the space with meaningless noise so they don't notice that thing. Is your mind doing the same, filling up your life with chatter while distracting you from the core of peace that is your true self? And are you complicit in that way of living when you're at work, filling the days with busy-ness? If you feel stressed and incomplete, then the answer, at least some of the time, might be 'yes'. But now you know it, you don't need to continue doing it mindlessly.

Today, I want to invite you back into balance at work and in life by embracing nothingness, just being. Of course, being isn't something you can find or practise, it isn't a thing, it's just who you are when you stop. Stop doing, stop thinking, stop chasing, just stop. There's no need to learn anything, gain anything or add anything to yourself. In fact, you need to let go. You need to allow yourself to just be you, and for that to be enough right now. This can sound a bit abstract or philosophical, so let me show you a simple, concrete way to try it out.

### Activity – Stop!

Set aside ten minutes today during which there is nothing you need to do. This is easier than it sounds: just create the time and let everything be for ten minutes. Unless your house is on fire (in which case I recommend rapid action), you will be fine, whatever your mind may say.

During that time, sit in a comfortable chair and move your attention to your breath. Let just the breath be enough activity for now, just keeping the body alive, being alive, without trying to become anything.

As you sit and breathe, notice how breath just happens, you don't even have to do it. Allow the breath to come and go like the sun does every day. When it comes, watch it, enjoy it. When it goes, watch and enjoy that.

Put down any effort to get something through this practice, through this moment, and allow this instant to be your entire life. Just sit, sink into the chair and be there as the witness of the breath right now.

As thoughts come and go, let them be, leave them alone if you can. They are not a problem, but they're not the focus right now, so allow them to come and go, but nothing more. Just be.

As your inner world begins to slow down, keep dropping all effort, all ambition, and just make this instant your whole focus. And when your time is up, notice how it's still now, and move back into activity when that seems right.

Balancing being and doing is crucial to being a healthy human being. No amount of doing can bring meaning into your life, even if your career is one that is thought of as something that makes a difference.

True meaning is knowing who you are in this moment, living as something more than a flurry of activity. And when you bring this balance and this meaning into your everyday work, then whatever you do, you will bring peace, creativity and quality into this world.

# WEEK 2

## Working Upside Down

Welcome to the beginning of this journey, which has a slightly different orientation than you may think. There is plenty of mindfulness teaching that explores the purpose of mindfulness practice in different contexts, including at work. These books can show you how to use mindfulness to become a better worker or manager, and that is a great thing, but our journey is different. For me, mindfulness – learning to live in the present moment – is not a tool for being a good person, it is the entire purpose of my life. All the things I do, like work and family, are opportunities to deepen my mindfulness practice, as well as places in which I can bring mindfulness, and peace, into the world.

This week, we will begin with this attitude in mind and you will quickly see how life can change when the challenges and opportunities of work become fuel for the deepening of your connection with this moment.

# Day 1: True Productivity

The concept of productivity is a well-worn one in Western culture. Work smarter, not harder, do more with less and get the most out of yourself every day. Seen this way, productivity is a measure of your output, combined with clear direction, and if you combine these two most of the time, you are a productive member of society.

But there are two levels of production: the outer and the inner. On an outer level, the work you do produces ideas, things and outcomes for those you serve. On the inner level, the way you engage with this instant produces an outcome too. For many people, the main inner outcome they produce is stress, excessive thinking and worry. And this happens for a very simple reason.

Your mind is obsessed with the future because it believes two things: that the present moment is not good enough and that salvation will come in the future. To achieve future salvation, your mind continuously plots your next steps, predicting what will lead to the happily ever after and then striving for it.

There are a couple of clear problems with this, the most obvious being that the future doesn't exist, so you will never find happiness there. The second thing is that there is no happily ever after, life is fluid and it continues to grow, develop and change. The only way to live happily is not ever after but right now, and the only way to do that is to embrace the movement of life, surfing the waves and loving it. You can't surf in still water, and there is no joy in stagnation, in maintaining things as they are, because it is against the way of nature. Everything is evolving, changing, developing or disappearing, and that is as it should be.

So while the intent of your mind is to find happiness through thinking, the only happiness comes from being here now, and it is the striving for something else that causes the stress that so many are in the grip of.

On the contrary, it is possible to work in such a way that you create an inner state of joy and peace, and this is true productivity. There are three simple steps to this way of working:

1) Engage fully with what is happening this instant.
2) Allow it to be exactly as it is.
3) Do whatever you can to make it better.

To produce an inner state worth celebrating, you need to be present, fully engaged in what you are doing now. Thinking about something else will take attention away from this instant, into thinking, which is the path to stress. As you notice what is happening now, your mind may start to label and complain about what is, which can create further problems. But if you allow what is, you can be there with it quite peacefully. And finally, as you watch closely from a place of peace, you will become aware of things that you could do to improve the situation, and you may find yourself doing them. Here is a simple way to test this process out at work, right here and now.

## Activity – True Productivity

Try this when you are doing a regular, repetitive task that you would normally avoid or dislike.

Before you start, bring your attention into your body by feeling yourself breathing in and out. Allow breath awareness to move your attention into the now.

As you do the task, pay close attention to everything you do. Feel every movement, notice the sounds produced and the sights you see. Be alert, attentive and deliberate in your movements.

Just for this instant, let the job be as it is. Be more interested in noticing what it is like to be doing this now than you are in whether it is good or bad. Allow this to be your whole world for a few moments and see what it is like to do the job without resisting it.

As you work, be watchful and notice any ways that the job could be improved. Is there a way to make it easier, safer or faster? Does working more slowly lead to a better result? Whatever you notice, put it into practice straight away if you can, or discuss it with work colleagues if you need to do that first. Of course, some workplaces aren't keen on changing things, but even so, the act of looking at the work in this way is its own reward.

Try doing a couple of jobs in this way today, and see how it changes your experience.

The change we are making here is radical. Instead of seeing work's job as being to make you happy, you are taking responsibility for your own enjoyment of life right now. This shift in responsibility moves your focus from the outer world to your inner experience, and it removes the expectation that some outside circumstance can make you happy. This is incredibly freeing, as the world cannot truly make you happy, real happiness comes from within, and when you embrace this wholeheartedly, work can resume its true purpose.

## Day 2: The Purpose of Work

On the surface, work has many purposes. There are the obvious ones, like making enough money to have food to eat and a place to live, and then there are more subtle ones, like making a contribution, building a career, being part of a team and doing something you love.

But from the perspective we are taking during this journey, these are all secondary to the one true purpose of work: to wake you up from the dream of thinking.

To call this existence a dream may be challenging at first, but if you pay close attention to your experience when you are caught by past and future thoughts, you will notice how dreamlike it can be.

My friend Cathy lives like that, completely lost in the thoughts that run through her head on repeat. I can tell because every now and then, her eyes glaze over and I can see that she is somewhere else. She's thinking, of course, thinking about before or after, but not here with me now. Her body is here, but her attention is elsewhere.

For me, on the other hand, work is a great adventure in the present moment, and a wonderful way to practise mindfulness. As I go through each day, challenges come to me and I sometimes find myself intensely mindful and alert, listening and looking carefully. At other times, I go to sleep too, and I find myself complaining, talking too much, making myself sound good when I talk to others. These are all signs that I am lost in the story of me, the self-image created from my imagined past and future.

You might say that past and future are real, but I can't find them, except as thoughts arising now. What else is there but this very instant?

And when I am lost in those stories, the stress I feel reminds me and demands that I return my attention to what is here now. I take a moment to go inside and feel what is arising in my body, to allow it to be, and I stay connected with that until it dissolves. I have the perfect job for that, and I always have. Even when I was delivering pizzas and building fences, each job was perfect for that stage in my life. What I do now may seem more 'meaningful' than those jobs, but really I am standing, walking, sitting, talking, listening – the same things as always.

Yesterday, I didn't like my job much, or my mind didn't. I wanted to stay home, to work somewhere else, to do something different. I felt tight in my chest and my thoughts were stressful. I felt a heaviness descend and work seemed to be the cause. But when I looked inside and just experienced that moment, without telling myself a story, I realised that I had been lost in my own stories, my own desire, and that I was resisting reality.

Sometimes, when I sit through meetings that seem pointless or deal with people who seem bureaucratic, I get into a mental fight with what's happening. Work doesn't cause this, but it does enlighten me to that pattern within me, and when I am aware of it, I can be mindful with it and it doesn't cause so many problems. What a relief!

Work can show you where you are stuck in a pattern of thinking, where your beliefs clash with reality and where you are resisting what is. Once you are aware of these habits, they will start to dissolve and your connection to this moment will deepen. So in some ways, the worse your job is from a conventional perspective, the better (and that doesn't mean you can't leave). If you embrace your work as a way to deepen your practice, the challenges become the most helpful part, and you can even look forward to being challenged and finding out a little bit more about yourself.

All of this discovery slowly erodes the false identity we have built around ourselves through years of thinking, talking and conditioning. And as the false erodes, you may just find out who you truly are.

## Activity – Discovering the False

The word false may seem a bit harsh here, but this activity will help you to identify everything that isn't you, but is part of your experience. And that's a big hint right there. Everything that is part of your experience isn't you!

Close your eyes for a moment and you will discover something interesting. There are two levels of experience: there is what happens and there is the one it happens to. Feel your breath coming and going and notice that there is the breath, and there's you, feeling the breath. Likewise there is sound and there is someone hearing sound, there are thoughts and someone who is aware of thoughts. And that someone, or something, is pure awareness.

Close your eyes again and ask yourself a simple question: Who am I? Notice all the answers your mind provides: 'I am

Jane Smith, primary school teacher at St. Mary's, divorced with three children . . .' etc. All of those descriptions are thoughts, stories based on memories of the past, of experiences you had and things you saw and heard. Things happened to you and your mind made sense of them by creating stories into which those events would fit. But who are you underneath all that?

Beneath all those thoughts, there is an alert, open awareness that watches everything that unfolds in your life. That awareness has always been with you, because, of course, it is you. Everything else is either an experience happening now, a projection or a memory.

So today, whenever you feel upset, angry, depressed or stressed at work, see what story, what false identity is operating. It is only when a part of your identity is challenged that these feelings arise, and in this, the seemingly stressful situations that arise at work can be a blessing in disguise as they show you where the false still lurks in you. And when you notice the false, you can quickly draw your attention back to the awareness that you are, and then work has done its job.

## Day 3: Working in Relationship

For most people, work is not a solitary pursuit, it is a team sport. When you arrive at your job each day, you probably are engaging in something that is reliant on, and affects, the lives and work of other people. And it seems, from my observations and what people tell me, that the biggest challenges (as well as the biggest thrills) at work come from the relationships we experience there. Whether those relationships are with customers, co-workers or others we meet along the way, these interactions provide rich food for our mindfulness practice, in the wonderful as well as the difficult moments.

Today, we will explore how relationships at work can be used skilfully to enjoy what arises and to deepen our awareness when difficulty enters our world.

When I sit down with my colleague Angie, it seems as if time had stopped, or that I wish it would. The conversation and the way she listens draws me into the present, and I find myself fully engaged, listening and delighting in the dialogue that arises. We each bring something different to the table and the experience is quite incredible. The enjoyment of the conversation makes me want to come closer to this moment. But when Jackie, who works in another team, speaks, I feel like my ego is bristling, standing up tall, getting ready to argue. We see the world differently and my mind sees this as a rare opportunity to argue, take a position and feel better than someone else. This feels quite awful.

It would seem that, if I wanted to be more mindful, I should avoid Jackie and spend more time with Angie, but mindfulness is about being present with what is, not trying to manipulate it to get more of what I want, and it turns out that Jackie has even more to give than Angie.

You see, when life is going well and people are being nice, the mind is getting what it wants and there is less resistance to what is. I say 'less' because the mind loves a fight and is never *completely* satisfied, is it? Your mind (and mine) are believers that the now isn't good enough and that the future will be better, so there's always room for improvement. But overall, the mind tends to quieten down at these times because things appear to be working, and it's fine to enjoy those times, as long as you stay alert. It's easy, however, to daydream your way along when life isn't pushing you too hard. And many unconscious mind patterns only get stirred up when you get to spend time with Jackie.

I'm sure you have a Jackie in your life, and at your job. Jackie might be a person, an organisation, a process or a system you have to work within. Jackie is anything (or anyone) that pushes your buttons, bring that unconsciousness to the surface and leads you into a state of resistance, or so it seems.

In fact, Jackie has nothing to do with these feelings, they arise because you want Jackie to be different than she is. You want her to be more . . . and less . . . and you believe, in that moment, that she is wrong and that she should change her ways. But there's a better way to work with what Jackie brings to your life.

### Activity – Mine

Close your eyes and remember a moment with Jackie that you experienced recently. Recall as much detail as you can and notice how your body and your mind respond to that memory.

Forget about Jackie for a moment. Feel your body from the inside instead. Identify the sensations that are arising and notice how much of your body they take up. Pick the strongest sensation and be intensely alert as you watch it, allowing it to be there.

As you do this, you may notice that the sensation changes, or it may stay the same, and either way is fine. We're not here to control the sensation but to feel it. That feeling is part of the present moment, so to resist it is to resist the now. Be mindful instead and embrace what is wholeheartedly.

Stay with this practice for as long as you would like, and return to it whenever you feel angry, upset or stressed this week.

Congratulations! You are learning to be mindful, to be peaceful, even when your mind and body are agitated. This skill means that, whatever happens in your life, it doesn't need to disturb your inner peace, and without the Jackies of your world, it would be much harder to learn this.

I have had many Jackies in my life (and I'm sure I have been one for someone else many times) and over the years, I find myself bothered by fewer things. Some still remain, seeming injustice and bureaucracy in particular, but the list used to be much longer and I always thought that it was *their* fault that I was upset. Not anymore.

You too can start to erase your list of gripes and buttons to be pushed by embracing challenging relationships at work. This will allow you to work more easily with people who seem difficult, and they will enable you to find peace in more challenging situations, until nothing remains but peace. But don't take my word for it, try embracing the feelings you have next time Jackie comes in or sends you an email. Soon you'll be thanking her (or him) for bringing just the right challenge for you to grow a little more.

# Day 4: Towards Perfection

It is in the nature of all creatures to strive for perfection, to keep evolving and improving in a seemingly endless cycle. And for human beings, it is possible to channel this natural urge so that it fuels our awakening into the now. Because of the intensity required by this search for perfection, it can be a wonderful way to bring energy to your practice.

Intensity? Striving? Search? These words may seem incompatible with mindfulness practice, which of course is all about allowing the present moment to be as it is, but there is another angle here, and it begins with an understanding of the nature of perfection.

The human mind continually projects perfection into the future, imagining that things will be perfect 'one day'. This view of perfection is as a stable place, in which everything is perfect and stays that way forever. Whether this is the desert island you want to retire to or the kingdom of heaven, the belief is the same: there is a permanent, stable state of perfection possible, but only in the future. But as mindfulness practitioners, the future doesn't exist, nor does the past, so the perfection we aim for is to be perfectly present right here and now, and to act out of that presence.

This means that, right now, we are aiming for perfect attention, and this practice continues forever, because as soon as you believe you attained perfection, you are lost in a thought, missing the mark once again. To stay connected to perfection, we have to stay alert.

At work, this practice can have two layers, and this is what makes work fun for me. The first layer is, as just mentioned, the continuous practice of trying to be mindful. The second layer is the ongoing attempt to perfect every process you do at work. To perfect a process, you need to be very alert, you need to observe it very carefully and you need to have a clear, open mind. You also need to start with the eyes of a beginner every time you do that task, otherwise you become conditioned to 'the way we do it' and you stop looking. If you are always looking for the next improvement, you will look with clarity and freshness, which isn't possible if you believe there's nothing to improve.

At my job, people tell me they are amazed at the questions I ask and the perspective I take on the work. I often ask things that seem obvious to me, but leave others floored. Why is this? There is nothing special about me, I promise, but because kind old masters have taught me how to sit and breathe and watch, I see what happens through the eyes of a child, with infinite curiosity. If you combine this with a level of expertise in the field, it adds up to something powerful and leads to improvements wherever I go. I don't make the improvements, I just look, the way my aunty looks at the crossword with intense presence until some complicated word comes tumbling out of her pen and on to the page. As I look without thinking, the observations are processed and my mind channels something simple and effective, more often than not. Others don't see this because they already 'know' what is wrong with the present moment and they're madly tumbling towards the future, trying to fix it.

If you observe with clear, peaceful awareness and combine this with your knowledge of your job, new ideas will come, and because they came out of what you *saw* instead of what you *believed*, they will perfectly fit the needs of the situation. Working in this way makes you better at your job and makes your workplace a better one, but more importantly, it will ground you in the peace that lies beyond thinking.

## Activity – The Only Perfection

Of course, on an external level, perfection is not possible. Every *thing* is impermanent, constantly changing, moving, coming or going. Nothing is static, so there is always room for growth and improvement.

On the inner level, though, there is something that is already perfect, something that cannot be improved in any way. *You.*

Close your eyes and find the only part of your experience that doesn't change, the only thing that doesn't ebb or flow, grow or shrink. The breath moves, the body changes, the mind changes, the world around you changes, and amidst all that, something stays the same. Awareness. The one constant is that you are there, watching, experiencing, noticing.

This awareness can't be adequately described in words, but if you sense behind your eyes you will notice that someone, or something, is watching. This awareness has no opinions, it has no beliefs, and it isn't harmed by emotions or thoughts, it just watches. And this awareness, the essence of you, is the only perfection. Everything else in your life can be improved, but awareness, which is another word for you, is unmovingly perfect.

To make true improvements, you must allow awareness to observe your work without being distracted by beliefs, ideas and memories. You must allow pure looking. And when you do this, you will bring benefits to your place of work and those you work with, but most of all, you will bring a deeper sense of joy and aliveness to your own life. And what could be better than that?

## Day 5: When Things (Seem to) Go Wrong

Unless you work in an enlightened workplace full of Zen masters, it is likely that you occasionally (maybe twenty times a day) come into conflict with those you work with. Maybe this is a manager who rules with an iron fist and a tiny mind, or maybe it is a co-worker who just clocks in every day, waiting for retirement and being present but not really accounted for. Or maybe you *are* that manager or that colleague; we all are sometimes. But regardless of the reason, the conflict that arises from time to time doesn't need to make work unpleasant or unproductive. In fact, these conflicts are rich opportunities for mindfulness practice.

You see, the problem with conflict is not the conflict itself, not the external happenings. The problem at the heart of conflict is inside, at the heart of *you*! Because when we argue with others, through words, actions or even by ignoring them, we are merely externalising our internal world as it is in that moment. Resistance starts within, and works its way out, just like every other state.

And at the core of resistance, there are a few interesting things happening. First, we believe that we know best, because resistance means that we are resisting life, arguing with it, mentally or out loud. In that moment, we know exactly how life is and we know how it should be, and in the gap between those two nows (the real and the imagined) resistance exists. And to know best, we must be lost in thinking, otherwise there is no way to believe that we are in possession of the truth. Actually, your mind whispers or shouts to you about how it should be, and when you believe that thought, resistance comes with it.

The second interesting thing that arises in the midst of resistance is a sort of tunnel vision, in which our perspective becomes narrower and we begin to see a very limited view of the world. We have only one worldview, and this becomes rigid, entrenched and immovable. Anything or anyone that threatens this worldview becomes the enemy, and we fight, directly or indirectly, by attacking that person or by talking about them to others. Whatever the symptom, the external appearance, the cause is the same.

These conflicts need not be earth-shattering to create stress and drama in your life. In fact, most dramas are petty, especially at work. Most are what is commonly called 'office politics', arguments about who doesn't clean the fridge, about who should get a new office or who doesn't pull their weight. Sit around any meeting table in the Western world (and probably the east now too), and you will see petty conflicts being played out as if they were a matter of life or death, because the mind loves them. That's right, your mind loves to be in conflict, because it allows you to define yourself by clearly demonstrating what you are not.

This is what happens when the mind is in control, and it feels pretty awful. There is often a sense of stress, a mild anxiety that accompanies this approach to life. And it is this stress that holds the key to unlocking the potential that conflict holds.

## Activity – Unlocking Conflict

Here is a simple set of practices to help you turn conflict into contentment. Make use of them whenever you find yourself lost in some drama at work, or anywhere else. You will find yourself relaxing into what is and calmly allowing situations to unfold, but you can still be assertive if needs be.

When you find yourself entering a state of resistance and you feel the stress that this evokes, move your attention immediately from the story of what happened, and what to do about it, to your breath. Don't pay attention to the situation for a moment (unless there is some action you need to take right now), be aware of your breath and your body instead.

Now take your attention to the stress itself. Feel exactly what it is like in this very instant, notice as much as you can about the way the stress arises, where it is in your body and how big it is.

As you make this attentional shift, your mind will not be happy. It will probably work very hard to bring your attention back to the story, wanting you to lose yourself in the drama. When this happens, the internal (and external) drama gains energy, (attention is energy after all) and the drama feeds the stressful feelings, which feed the drama. It's a perfect circle!

Breaking free of this is not easy at first, because the mind has so much momentum and we have trusted it for so long. But keep coming back to your breath, your body and the emotions that go with the drama. Stay alert, be curious and watch. And see what happens next.

Breaking this cycle of drama is quite a project, not because it's complicated, but because the mind is seductive, and drama is addictive. But like any other addiction, it isn't really satisfying, it's just a habit. So this week, when you find yourself wanting to buy into the everyday work drama, come back to your body and be curious with the feelings. Direct experience is the path to freedom, and when you do this, the drama and the stress are helping you to become more present, which is a wonderful thing to happen.

## Day 6: Growing You

As you have already discovered, mindfulness places a great emphasis on the present moment. Sometimes it seems as if this leaves no place for learning from past experience, but today you will see how the past can be dealt with mindfully, bringing several benefits. First of all, this approach will allow you to learn from the past without any need for guilt, stress, sadness or anger, you will be able to coolly assess what happened and learn all you can. Second, you will be able to see what happened more clearly when you are not so caught up in your mind's story of what happened and *what should have happened.* This makes it easier to understand the real situation, without it being clouded by judgements.

But most of all, this method of learning, without relying on story, will allow you to learn in a state of peace and joy, and to focus on learning as it's happening *now*, rather than being lost in the past. This is an important distinction.

Being lost in the past means that your whole attention is absorbed in the mental movies that play in your mind.

When those movies play, your eyes glaze over and you are no longer there, except for your body. You have probably seen people lost in their minds like this, like a real-life version of zombie shows or films. When you meet someone who is lost like this, you can wave your hands in front of them, ask if they have ever been to the moon and they will continue to stare dead straight. And when you are the one who is lost, it is like being asleep and dreaming, the images seem so real. Of course, you have some awareness that they are memories, but your body may respond as if they were real. And the images are often not pure memory, but memory accompanied by a running mental commentary of the story your mind is telling. So as you see the image of your manager talking about cutting your budget, the thought 'he doesn't care, it's all about making himself look good' may occur in your mind, bringing a sense of frustration, powerless and anger with it.

Your mind will then want to project another movie, this time a version of the future, in which you confront the nasty manager, give him the rounds of the kitchen and get your budget back. This is another version of the 'happily ever after' stories that the mind looks to for salvation, and when your mind is in control, there is loss of curiosity about what happened and what might be possible. There is one preferred storyline and you are pushed towards it, at all costs. And when it doesn't come to fruition, the crash is even worse.

Of course, the outside world may not agree with your mind's version of what should happen; in fact, it's highly unlikely that it will. And as the outside world continues to thwart your mind's desires, more frustration, anger and sadness will accumulate. This is a vicious circle.

The alternative, using past experience to deepen yourself, is much more simple and straightforward. I call this way of living 'growing you' because you are using the nutrients that life gives you (even if it smells like compost) to nourish you, deepen your roots and allow you to blossom.

## Activity – Growing You

Take a moment to remember a big challenge you confronted at work in the past. Think of something you would gladly have escaped from and avoided if someone had given you the chance, and write it down on a piece of paper as follows:

*A challenge I wanted to escape from was . . .*

Sit with that statement for a moment, then close your eyes and take your attention into your body. Bring up the memories you have of that time and see if you can reflect on them without being drawn into stories about what was right or wrong, what should or shouldn't have happened. Just allow those memories to come through your awareness now and make space for them to be with you in this moment.

Open your eyes and grab your pen again, this time completing the following sentence:

*The top three things I gained from that challenge were:*

1) _____

2) _____

3) _____

Write these as quickly as you can manage, then take a few moments to let them sink in. What were the hidden gifts of that situation? What did it give you that you wouldn't have otherwise?

Now finally, close your eyes again and imagine how this situation could have been if you had not internally resisted what was going on, if you could have stayed present and simply allowed it to progress as it did, responding in the best way you could. What would the experience have been like without your story? How would you have felt outside work, on weekends? Perhaps they were the times when you were stewing over the situation and what would happen next. What if you could have simply dealt with each challenge, without any mental arguments about what should be happening instead?

The point of this exercise is not to beat yourself up over your lack of presence, but simply to see the futility and the cost of resisting what is. Inner resistance does not change the situation; indeed it often traps us in a conditioned response that perpetuates it. So this week, try working with these situations, not against them, and see how your life begins to change.

## Day 7: Learning to Pick Up and Drop

If you watch most humans at work (including me sometimes), you will notice something that seems odd when you examine it. Most humans are thinking about something else while they are at work. They are thinking about the weekend, or what's for dinner, and so they are not fully *there* as they work. Paradoxically, many humans think about work most when they *aren't* there! They spend the weekends (which they were fantasising about at work) complaining to others about the boss, talking about their work problems and feeling stressed about their to-do list.

How interesting that we tend to pay attention to the area of life that we can't do anything about right now, while ignoring the one thing we can influence. Watch and listen to people at work and you will see and hear this pattern in action.

So, as today is the last day of this week, I wanted to share my tips for leaving work at work and leaving home at home, learning to pick up and drop. This is something I discovered the hard way.

Many years ago, I spent lots of time outside of work thinking and talking about work. I was friends with colleagues and we would catch up on weekends, discussing the week's events and making dramas in our collective minds. We loved those dramas, as they made us feel closer, but often I got to work on Monday feeling as if I hadn't left, and then I spent the week waiting for the weekend.

A few years later, the opposite happened. When my son Liam was a baby, I felt guilty about going to work, missing out on family time and not being there to help out. So when I was at work, I was often either scheming about how to become self-employed or I was thinking about home, feeling bad about not being there.

Both these scenarios were the same at heart: I was mentally (and sometimes verbally) complaining about my reality and demanding something different. In both situations the arguments only served to create stress, sadness and upset. They were completely counterproductive.

Today, I went to work and I loved it. As soon as I rode out the gate on my bike, I left home at home. I arrived at work clear-headed and the day was amazing, I walked, talked to people and ran into old friends in the park. It was hot and steamy, and then it rained, which is rare where I live. And as I rode home in the rain, getting soaking wet in the heat, work evaporated like the rain on the hot roads. It's gone as I sit here and type.

In one sense, work dropped away because it's no longer here, but I prefer to think of it in another way. I picked up something else, which was the ride home, dinner, playing, reading, and now sitting here typing. It's much easier to pick up something new than to try to drop the past. And here is a simple ritual you can use to let the past stay in its place, and to be fully here instead.

## Activity – Picking Up, Putting Down

Life is a continuous movement, from one thing to another, that's why they call it 'life'! And in your experience too, there is a constant changing of what is to what was. If you step straight into this flow and stay there, you will experience the smooth flow that is possible when you move along as life intends.

Close your eyes and feel your breath and you can experience this directly. The in breath is important, and it feels good, then it's over. There is a pause, like your commute home from work, and then the out breath comes, and that's lovely too. Here comes the in breath again, right on time, and so it continues.

Try using breath awareness to bring your attention to what you are doing right now. As you pick up the present moment with your awareness, you will notice that the past and the future naturally drop away. Feel your breath and be alert and aware as you do whatever is required right now. Then, as you move on to a new activity, shift your awareness again, so that you are always focused on what is, right here and now.

When thoughts about the past or the future arise, let them be there, but try not to lose yourself in them. Keep most of your attention on what you are doing now, allowing those thoughts to bubble along in the background as they wish. Try living like this over the next 24 hours and see what it feels like to flow smoothly along with the current of life.

Learning to pick up and drop is quite a challenge at first, because it goes against all our conditioning, but try it in small doses over the coming days and weeks. You will start to discover that living in this way requires more attention, but creates less stress and needs less effort overall, because you only need to do this one thing well now. And just dealing with this will make your life incredibly simple and immensely enjoyable.

# WEEK 3

## Embracing Difficulty

Nobody seeks out difficult times, but it seems that the path for every human involves numerous challenges, and when those days (or weeks, months, years) arrive, we share a common instinct to escape. Quite naturally, we want to avoid these trials so we can continue to live a comfortable, easy life, but often this isn't possible. In hindsight, you may be able to see the gifts that certain challenges gave you, but in the moment this is impossible to predict. All we know is that it hurts, it's hard, and that we want our mums!

But challenges, in fact, have many things to teach you, and they can make you more mindful, present and peaceful, if you treat them the right way. And if a challenge is happening now, then it is an inescapable part of this moment, so fighting with it will lead to predictable results: stress, anger, sadness, despair. Embrace that same challenge as an opportunity and you will feel a greater sense of aliveness, alertness and purpose. Stay curious, open and interested, and you will see those challenges become wonderful gifts, right before your eyes.

This week, we dive into the muddy world we all sometimes land in after hitting one of the bumps on life's road. The activities and the teachings will show you just how to get unstuck while learning and growing as a person through these difficulties. They'll happen anyway, so you might as well enjoy them.

# Day 1: Stuck in the Mud

I am a massive fan of books on productivity and effectiveness, and I love the simple skills and tools that so many authors and companies share. I would never think of most of them and I find them hugely valuable, most of the time. Some days, though, I feel like I'm stuck in the mud and I can't get moving. On those days, I don't want to apply those good ideas or stick with helpful habits, I just want to crawl under my desk and read a good book. Maybe you have days like this too.

A couple of weeks ago I had a day just like this, something that seems to happen every few months. On this particular day, the mud felt especially thick and the effort to get moving was quite something. And this is where conventional wisdom seems to cause more harm than good. The standard advice when the mud is thick is to go back to your good habits, put your shoulder to the wheel and muscle your way out. This might work in the short term, but it's a bit like playing on after a few painkillers to mask your sprained ankle, or putting on a brave face when what you need is some time alone.

I perfected the brave face over many years, and this is my first instinct when I notice the mud, the feeling of listlessness, of pointlessness that saps all energy for forward motion. But as I have gone deeper into mindfulness practice, I started doing something completely different: sinking deeper into the mud. I began to wonder if those feelings were in fact a signal, a message to which I should listen, like pain in that sprained ankle.

So as I sat in a cafe on that day a few weeks back, I went to my breath and felt the feelings fully. I allowed myself to experience every part of that moment, without trying to change a thing. My mind kept trying to explain the feelings away or decide what to do about them, but I left those thoughts alone and let the sensations themselves tell me what to do next.

Once I got comfortable in the mud, things got interesting, as ideas and possibilities began to flow into my awareness. Within an hour of that, I had sent an email and made three phone calls that led to a significant change in my work situation. These changes were things I had not considered until the mud gave me a gentle nudge, and they have worked out to be amazing. If I had tried to push my way through, I would have missed them.

As it turned out, the mud was actually quicksand and I had been trying to thrash my way through it. You probably know that, in quicksand, you should lie back, relax into it, spread your arms wide and wait for a friend with a rope! When you relax into it, the quicksand will (apparently) support your weight. Fight with it and you will only sink deeper. So as I sat with it, I was supported, and I realised that I needed help from a couple of friends, who were able to support this new direction. Here is a step-by-step guide to what I did that day, so you can try it when you feel stuck at work.

## Activity – Getting Unstuck

When it comes to getting unstuck, there are only two steps that I recommend: sit and wait. This may sound passive and unhelpful, but let me explain a little further using the example I mentioned earlier.

When I realised I was stuck, there was one clear sign: a heavy, hollow feeling in my chest. I also felt lethargic and a little bit grumpy, but that feeling in my chest was enough to let me know that something was off kilter. After fighting it for a while, I decided to go into the feeling more deeply, and to see what it had to tell me.

I went to a cafe and ordered an espresso, picking a corner table to sit. As I waited, I took my attention to that sensation, feeling it fully. At the same time I took a piece of paper and a pen and started writing. I didn't aim to write about anything in particular, but just to write.

As I wrote, I was as mindful as I could be of my breath and my body, especially that feeling. And as I wrote, insights began to occur to me as thoughts, leading to the new ideas I mentioned before. So that stuckness became a great gift-giver, and things became better than they had been before it arose.

So, to summarise, that process goes like this:

- Order coffee (optional).
- Direct attention to the feeling inside you.
- Write whatever comes to mind.
- Wait and see what insights arise.

So if you get stuck today, or this week, or this month, try a new approach. Try lying back in the quicksand, experiencing it fully, and seeing what insights bubble to the surface when you stop fighting with what is.

# Day 2: Why?

When difficulty arises, our first question is usually: 'Why?' Why did this happen to me? What is the purpose of it all and why can't it be happening to somebody else? But if we want to become truly mindful and make the most of every opportunity that life gives us, we need to ask a better question, or at least a different sort of why.

Ask yourself, 'Why do I need this experience now?' and you may get a different sort of answer, one that makes you appreciate the opportunities hidden in the challenges you face.

This isn't instinctive for humans. We usually act as if the universe is making a mistake, as if the world around us – which has the intelligence to manage the climate, the oxygen levels in the atmosphere – and keep the earth in the right orbit for you to walk to your meeting without being thrown up into the atmosphere, stuffed up when it came to this. Maybe it was a job you missed or a pay rise you didn't get, or maybe it is the behaviour of someone in your office. But whatever it is, the world is giving you that experience now because that is what you need, and that doesn't mean you have to stay there one second longer.

But this can become an argument about whether things should be happening or not, which is a massive waste. Instead, you can notice one simple fact: it *is* happening. That thing you don't like, that you want to get rid of, to change, it is as it is right now. Simple.

And once we accept the *isness*, as Eckhart Tolle calls it, of this moment, we have only two options: fight it or work with it. Fight and you get stress, a more and more closed view of the world and a lifetime of frustration. Work with it and who knows? Maybe you will discover something wonderful hiding in this seeming catastrophe.

A few years ago, I went for a job I thought I wanted, two jobs, actually, in a short space of time. I didn't get either. Ten years ago, this would have been devastating, but having a little sanity, I have realised that I don't pick jobs. In reality, they pick me, and they always know best. So I was able to keep enjoying what I was doing and, by chance, I was asked to do one of those jobs for six months. A few weeks in, I could see that this wasn't the job for me. It just didn't match my best skills or my favourite tasks, and others are much better at doing those things, so I don't have to.

The key here is to drop all the whys and pick up the whats. What can I do to improve this? What opportunities does this give me? What can I contribute from where I am today? These questions can unlock the potential that remains untapped when we try to figure out why.

## Activity – From Why? to What?

Take a moment now to see what happens when you make this simple shift. Bring to mind a situation you have been trying to mentally pull apart and understand, something that has really been bothering you. Try dropping all your why questions and write down the following instead:

- What would happen if I accepted the situation fully?
- What could I contribute from where I am?
- What would help me to make the best possible contribution?

- What benefits could there be in working with what is happening?
- What are the possible costs?

Of course, this does not mean going with something that is unethical, or wrong in your eyes, nor doing anything that compromises your integrity. It simply means accepting that the situation is as it is, and working constructively to be as helpful and kind as you can be.

This might mean being assertive and telling someone their behaviour is not OK, or it might mean leaving your job. But most often, these steps are smaller and simpler, but they can still create radical change.

But the most radical change, the one worth celebrating, is that your attention has moved, from thinking about the past and the future, to being completely present with what is. There is nothing more important than making this shift right now.

Using this simple movement, from why to what, you can change your entire world this instant. You can unstick yourself, releasing energy to do something positive in the world, instead of clogging it with the negativity of resistance. How cool is that?

## Day 3: Difficult Bosses

Seemingly, difficult bosses are everywhere. They inhabit every workplace, school and family home in the world. They're in shops, on buses and on TV. Sometimes they're even looking us in the mirror when we brush our teeth! In other words, all of us can seem difficult at times, but there are bound to be a few people in your life who have a special gift for pushing your buttons, and often they seem to be the one in charge! You know the ones, they'll have you totally lost in resistance, in a mental story, before they have finished their first sentence of the day. To the mind, these people are the pits!

But to the mindfulness student, they are incredibly helpful, because nothing can change them! Why is this a good thing? Because it leaves all the responsibility for your happiness with you, right where it belongs. When we argue with what is and we ask reasonable people to change in order to make us happy, they often comply. This is nice in the short term, but it leaves the cause of the unhappiness – our addiction to thinking – untouched. But difficult people will never comply, especially when they have power in the workplace. And for this we should be grateful.

When your boss won't change, and you know they won't, then you have a simple choice. You can either dig in and keep arguing, or you can take responsibility for your own happiness. And if you have a difficult boss, finding happiness is surprisingly simple, especially at work. There are only two steps that I use.

Firstly, don't try to change them. It's impossible anyway, so don't waste any energy on it, not one kilojoule. Secondly, when they speak, be quiet and listen mindfully. That's all. When that person is talking, can you just listen without judging? Can you be there as mindfulness, as the watcher of it, without getting lost in your story? Can you take care of your own inner space and leave them to be their own person?

With practice you can, if you drop the idea that you know how they should be different.

The saviour mentality is embedded in every human mind, and so we can be tempted to try to 'change' or 'fix' others by telling them what to do different, or by arguing with what they are doing now. Some of us are subtle in this, some direct, but the results are roughly comparable. This urge is often even stronger if that person is your boss.

A friend of mine recently told me about some drama that happened at their work, because everyone was trying to change the boss. That person used power as a tool to try to control people, and they rebelled, but they responded by trying to use power to change the boss! This deteriorated into a power struggle in which both 'sides' used less than ethical tactics to try to get the change they wanted, everyone was exhausted and things got worse. And then the boss left anyway. This is a common story.

The mind seeks control when it sees something it does not like, and these attempts to control almost always lead to resistance and push back. So the pattern of mind the boss was lost in became that of the whole office, everyone trying to make reality change by manipulating the people around them. But reality, even when it comes in the form of a difficult boss, always knows best. That doesn't mean you can't give feedback, or make suggestions, or leave. But it does mean that, if you want to be happy, you need to take care of your inner world yourself. And to do this, you need to leave others to their own journey.

## Activity – Just Listen!

Pick someone at work who tends to be argumentative, someone you find it difficult to deal with, (if this is your boss, then all the better) and the next time you have a conversation with them, try doing the following:

- As they start talking, take your attention into your body and concentrate on listening intently. Don't think about what they say, just be there and hear them fully. Don't do anything to change them in any way, just let them be exactly as they are right now.
- Be the space. Stay in your business. Be the witness of what is happening. Notice how you can feel your body and listen, all at the same time, and feel the peace of that. How wonderful to be alive in this moment!
- If the person asks you a direct question, answer it honestly, then go back to listening. If you don't know the answer, tell them the truth, then go back to listening.
- Notice how it feels to be the listener, to be the one who is completely available and open, without an ounce of judgement.

Often, something strange happens when you are there as complete openness for the other person: they begin to change. Many seemingly difficult people actually feel quite uncomfortable within themselves. They, like everyone else, want someone to love them for who they are, for someone to see them without judgement.

And to be with someone in a state of mindfulness is the ultimate act of love. Seeing someone from there, from a completely non-judgemental space, can lead to surprising changes in the other person. In my life, I see this all the time. People around me are waking up, growing and changing before my eyes, and I do nothing but watch and listen.

This may sound a little cosmic, and it is. But try it this week with those you find difficult at work and at home. Run it as an experiment, and see what happens. You might be surprised!

And if your boss seems to be the difficult one, give them this open attention too and see what happens. They may not change, but your experience of being with them will surely become more pleasant when you step out of resistance and into the open space of awareness.

## Day 4: Big Challenge, Big Growth

Today I had an interesting experience at work: I felt the urge to back away from a challenge. There's something brewing (perhaps) that I would rather avoid, and so my mind seeks to try to make sure that things go the way they 'should'. Breathing in, though, I notice a couple of things that make the picture a little different. Firstly, all that future is imaginary, it simply doesn't exist. Even work doesn't exist for me when I'm not there, except as a thought in my head. The second thing I notice is that the situation, even if it follows my mind's imaginary course, is not a problem. A challenge maybe, but never a problem.

What's the difference between a problem and a challenge? Your attitude. A challenge is lugging heavy weights around at personal training; a problem is lugging heavy buckets of water out of your flooded house. A challenge makes you stronger and is fun; a problem (according to the mind) shouldn't be happening.

For us humans, there is a fundamental disconnect between what we want and what we need. We need to be challenged, to grow, to improve. We want to be comfortable, and for everything to work as we wish. Today we will explore how to flip this approach, so that the bigger the challenge is, the more rewarding the situation becomes, and the more mindful *you* become.

I realised a few years ago that, when it comes to deepening my mindfulness progress, difficulty is much more helpful than comfort. When life is comfortable, we can happily daydream, drift away into thought and lose awareness of the present moment. If our thoughts about the past and the future are pleasant, they can seem comforting, enjoyable and fulfilling, which can lead us away from this instant.

Discomfort, on the other hand, doesn't leave you much room for this daydreaming. Thoughts become stressful and so it is much easier to live in this instant than to be lost in stories. During the honeymoon, you can happily imagine your life together (rather than living your *actual* life together now), but during the bitter divorce, you may experience a profound deepening of your awareness, because thoughts are too painful to get lost in for long.

And life at work is the same. The bigger the difficulty you face, the bigger the need to be present and work with it. If you are present with the challenge, it can't turn into a problem. A problem only occurs after the fact, through thinking. Even the thought 'problem' must be a comment on the past, because you cannot think in real time, there is always some delay. If, instead, you are engaged with the challenges fully, then work becomes tremendously enjoyable, and the harder it is, the better.

## Activity – Big Challenge, Big Fun

Things only feel like problems because when we think about how the future may turn out, they feel serious and important. When you play a game that has nothing riding on it, then the more challenging it is, the more fun it is. When I play basketball, the tougher the other team, the better, but when my mind runs wild at work, worrying about the future, that fun is obscured.

Bring to mind a challenge in your work life right now. Picture the situation in your mind, making sure to pick something specific. As you imagine what you may have to do, make one small change. Imagine that there was no future, no repercussion possible from this activity or event. What if it was just a role play, a simulation, a game? Imagine yourself working on the challenge with this spirit. What difference would it make?

Now add another twist to the situation. Imagine that your only goal in the situation was to be mindful in every instant. What if your primary focus was on staying alert and awake rather than drifting into thinking? What if the outcome of your efforts was secondary, but the quality of your attention was primary?

This activity gives a glimpse into a different way of living and working with challenges, but why stop there? This week, take the chance to experiment with this way of approaching challenges, whatever they are. Whether you are cleaning the house, running up a hill or having a conversation with a colleague, bring this spirit of alertness and challenge into your life and you may well discover that your so-called problems were but a figment of your imagination.

# Day 5: Finding Closeness in Conflict

Conflict is an interesting word. Most people say they don't like it, but it happens nonetheless. It appears to drive us apart as humans when this happens, and workplace conflict is no different. But today, I want to suggest that we recycle the word conflict and turn it into something more helpful. The word 'con' in Spanish means 'with', and I suggest that we use the word 'closeness' instead.

After all, when we are in 'conflict', isn't the problem that we're a little too close? When I feel in conflict with another, it's usually because I am mentally trying to live their life for them, thinking about what they *should* be doing differently. I have left my body, my experience, to speculate about how the other person should live right now, and it feels uncomfortable for us both. Of course, the other person usually resists this, as do I, and so the external world becomes conflictual too.

Lucky for me, this very rarely happens anymore because I have no interest in how others live their lives, that's up to them. I am still interested in closeness, but I want to be close to *me*, not to you. What I mean is that I don't enjoy mentally living your life for you, but I love being present in my body, here and now. From that place of presence, I also deeply enjoy spending time with you, listening to you and playing together, but my primary relationship is with me.

The reason for this approach is twofold. Firstly, I noticed how stressful it is to spend time and energy planning what other people should do next. I slipped into this trap a few days ago, believing I know how a recruitment process at work should be done, even though it's not my job. The result? Stress, frustration and some tension. Secondly, I have realised that I am the only person I ever truly live with. Others come and go from my presence, but I'm always here with my own body and mind. And when I returned to focusing on this primary relationship in the situation mentioned above, I realised that I need to let go of the outcome my mind is projecting, I need to leave it alone and return to my own life, typing these words right now. *That* life is simple and straightforward, while the other is stressful and painful. Which would you prefer?

Imagine if every scrap of external conflict became a signal to return to your inner world and get back in touch with you. Imagine if every time you thought 'he should just' or 'she shouldn't have', it reminded you to go back to living *your* life, experiencing *your* world, right now.

## Activity – Returning to You

Perhaps today, or this week, you have found yourself out gallivanting in the worlds of other people. Luckily, you can return to you in an instant and it's enjoyable as well as simple.

Start by closing your eyes and giving your physical body some attention. Where is the stress of the week stored? Where do you feel tight, tense, contracted? Direct your attention to those areas as you notice your breath flowing in and out. You might want to let your shoulders drop on each out breath, just as a little gift to your body.

Smile and keep breathing as you keep noticing your inner world as it is right now. The act of paying attention is all that matters, there is no need to change even one little thing. Be with your body as it is now and you will experience a slowing down, a settling into the body.

When you discover stronger feelings of tension or stress, stay with them for a few minutes, bringing clear, alert awareness to them. Experience those feelings directly, letting them be exactly as they are. Congratulations, you have returned to you!

It's hopeless to try to control others, either mentally or verbally. Even if it works on an external level, it is exhausting, debilitating and corrosive to relationships. And at work it is easy to fall into this trap whenever you think a colleague, a partner or a manager should do things differently. Watch what happens next as your mind tries to draw you into an examination of what that person *should* be doing. If you follow your mind down the rabbit hole, you will find yourself deep in a closed in, difficult world. You may also find yourself behaving in ways that are not helpful.

But once you are aware of this process taking place, it is much easier to sidestep it. All you need to do is to notice yourself caught in this pattern and to shift attention from your story of the other to your inner experience. And it's quite amazing how such a minor shift can cause such radical changes.

## Day 6: Skilful Reflection

If mindfulness is all about now, then it can't possibly help us to learn from the past, right? This is a question I get fairly regularly (according to my mind, which is fairly unreliable) and I usually give a similar answer: even reflection happens now.

Because mindfulness is not a philosophy, a belief that 'it's always now', it's simply the observations from a lifelong science experiment with one question: Is it still now? Many people seem to see this as some sort of belief system, but if you just pay attention to when it always is, you will see that the past and the future aren't concrete things, they're thoughts. Thoughts that happen now.

In fact, the only reason we need to use terms like 'now' is because us humans get confused. My dog doesn't need that concept; for him, it's either food time now or it's not, and if not, it's sleep time now. But because we have this idea that past and future are real, and even that they're *more* important than the only time you actually live, we need to talk about the present moment.

In your workplace, you will probably notice this pattern as clear as day. Everything revolves around what happened yesterday and what we're going to do tomorrow to get a better result. This is not a problem, and you don't need to make it *your* way of living at work, you can chart a different path.

When the time comes to learn from the past, or from the thoughts I have in my mind that speak of the past, I generally do it with ease. In fact, I don't do it at all, I just notice what insights come out. In Zen, they say that, like food, our experience should be completely digested, it should become so integrated into ourselves that it is inseparable from who we are. And like digestion, this process should be unconscious, it should happen without thinking.

And so, good reflection begins during the experience itself, not afterwards. Mostly, people are distracted as they do things, and so they lack a deep awareness of the process. Skilful reflection, though, involves bringing as much awareness and alertness as possible into the moment of action, as if you were watching yourself perform it. In this way, you can learn deeply without even knowing it, the same way you start to understand the patterns of a game if you watch it closely for hours, or the way weather watchers learn the nuances of the clouds simply by watching.

If you aren't awake as you work, how can your 'memory' be trusted to help you to learn from the past? Those memories will be seen through the lens of your story about that experience, and this clouds your vision. Without clear seeing in the moment, we are looking at blurry photographs for evidence, and our memories can't really be trusted.

So part one of reflecting skilfully at work is being present in the action itself. The second part is to build time into your daily work to sit quietly and breathe. This is especially helpful if you have a dilemma or a decision to make at work, just sit with it, let it digest and trust yourself to find the best path forward without great strain or effort.

## Activity – Reflecting Now

Try this two-step process either in your daily activities or at work. Pick something that you do a few times a day and take a mindful breath or two before performing the task each time today. Bring attention to the activity itself, being present and alert as you do it.

Then, a few times throughout the day, take thirty seconds to just breathe, relax and allow your mind and body to process what has happened today so far. Write down any learnings that present themselves during or after these periods of quiet reflection.

This may seem overly simple (most powerful tools are), but you will be surprised to learn how much these practices can change your life. As I work each day, I pay as much attention as I can muster to each task, and it's almost as if I am observing myself doing my work. Then, several times throughout the day, I go for a mindful walk or spend some time quietly breathing, without doing anything in particular. I might spend up to ten minutes doing this, but it may be as short as thirty seconds to a minute.

This resets my attention and allows anything I missed earlier in the day to be processed, and I often notice ideas for improvements bubble to the surface when I stop doing and allow myself to be. I work in a pretty standard office environment, so I will sometimes walk down the street to do this, or put my headphones on to block out the noise.

People often say that I am 'creative' or that I come up with good ideas out of left field, but I notice that I never 'come up with' these thoughts, they happen to me when I am still. Others may have them too, but how could they hear them amidst all that mental noise?

This simple process is the antidote to the busy checklist culture that increases stress continuously in our workplaces, and you can start practising it right now.

# Day 7: No Difficulty Now

When people tell me about stressful events they have experienced at work, I sometimes ask two questions that can illuminate the inner workings of stress. The first question is: 'How long did that experience take?' That argument with your manager, the rudeness of your colleague, how long did it last in minutes and seconds? The second question is: 'And how much time have you spent thinking about it?'

Think of a recent drama in your work life and ask yourself these two questions. What were your answers? Often, people tell me that they even lasted less than five minutes, sometimes even less than five seconds! The mind may say that it has been happening for months, but in reality this means that several shorter events happened and the mind weaved them into one story. Look at each situation in isolation and you will see its true duration, which is usually quite short. But the time spent replaying it and dissecting it is often many many hours. Why do we do this to ourselves? We don't.

*You* don't inflict this on yourself, your mind does it to you, for your own good of course! Your mind believes that the future is where happiness will be found because this moment is not quite good enough. And your mind sees the past as the key to unlocking this great future. If you understand the past and figure out how to do things better in the future, that happy day will come. And from this viewpoint, pulling apart small events that seem to have large significance makes perfect sense, it's important. Watch the news and you'll see how the analysis of small things can be made to sound big and important, even if the big discussions of last month can barely be remembered.

And just as you will see on the news, where the amplification of small dramas prevents us from taking notice of the things that are actually important right now, often this mental process actually *reduces* your ability to improve the situation at your workplace. By the time you return, you may have spent so much time and energy analysing events that you have only a little energy left for your actual work. But if you learn how to move your energy from what was to what is, you may discover that, apart from making life more fun, you might also uncover some innovative solutions to those problems.

### Activity – What is the Problem This Very Instant?

I find it useful to ask myself and others what the problem is in this instant, especially when stress is arising. This question can help us to notice the difference between what the mind *says* is a problem and what is actually important right this instant.

We can take this a step further by adding a couple of extra questions that can unlock both your energy and your enthusiasm for making things better right now.

Start by bringing to mind a situation that has been bothering you lately. Picture it in detail and notice how your mind and body react to those memories.

Ask yourself these questions in order, taking some time to allow each one to answer itself, and for that answer to sink in.

- What is the problem this very instant? Not in five seconds or five hours or five years, but now?
- What can be done about the situation *now*?

- Where is the problem? Is it in your reality right now, or in your mind as a thought?

Take your time with the questions and beware of your mind trying to hijack the process and justify its position. If there are practical answers to question two, then do them straight away. If there is action to be taken, take it, then forget about it and move on. This is the path of peace.

Try asking these three questions whenever you get lost in a mental problem at work this week. Find out whether it is possible for a problem to exist *outside* of your mind. I haven't found any yet!

So here is the trick, the key to a content, peaceful experience at work everyday. Whenever a challenge/problem seems to arise, either do something (take action), or forget about it. If there's nothing you can do about it now, put energy into things you *can* improve right now. If there's something you can do, take action straight away and see what happens. Do your very best in the moment of action, then leave it alone.

You can never control the outcome, the only thing you have some control over is the process, the way you do your work or take action in the moment. What happens after that is a mystery until it happens, then it becomes the past, inevitable in hindsight!

Taking ownership of the mystery, as if your hands are on the universe's steering wheel, is a great way to stress yourself out. After all, you can't even make your heart beat one more time if it doesn't want to, so what hope have you of engineering an outcome in the world *outside* you? Close to zero.

But you can take action with awareness, mindfulness and quality, and this is a wonderful outcome in and of itself, a gift to you and the world around you.

# WEEK 4

## Working in Balance

The human race is grossly out of balance. We are swimming in technology, tactics and inspirational books showing us how to get more things done. But take a cold hard look at the last hundred or so years of our history and ask yourself: 'Is not getting enough done our biggest problem?'

Industrialisation has allowed us to do significantly more than ever before. More polluting, more killing, more stressing, more destruction, more logging, more money, more inequity, more oppression. Do we really need more?

This week, I want to ask some hard questions and get you to consider some countercultural perspectives. Instead of doing more, perhaps we should do less but enjoy it more. Less activity, more attention. Less stress, more peace. Less stuff, more creativity.

The search for more is an external one; it involves looking for experiences, resources, status and other 'things' from the external world. The search for less is an inner one; it involves looking inside, dropping anything unnecessary and discovering your own core of peace and contentment.

Amusingly, this peace is what everyone is seeking when they look for more! They believe that a little more of something will fill the hole and make them feel complete as human beings. But the only way to be complete is to stop searching, at which point you'll discover that everything you were seeking out there is already in here!

So stay open, even if your mind rebels. Keep reading even if you feel challenged, and email me – oli@ peacethroughmindfulness.com.au – if you want to talk about it. Above all, test out what I say and see if it fits, not with your *beliefs*, but with your *experience*.

## Day 1: But Why Do It in the First Place?

My work allows me to visit several offices through the course of each day. I see plenty of people who believe that Productivity = Tasks Completed / Time Spent. Get lots done quickly and you are a productive member of society. This ignores a fundamental question, though: Why are you doing that anyway?

Are the things you are doing leading to the creation of a better world for you and others, or are they a means to an end? Is your energy aligned with your purpose as a person, with the kind of life you wish to live? Does your work bring peace into the world, or are you just doing?

My friend Janet has this formula worked out. The more crosses through her to-do list there are at 5.06, the better the day was. She thinks I'm lazy, that I don't work hard enough, and that my way of working is a little unsettling (but she's very nice about it). Yet Janet is missing a little secret I discovered a few years back.

I discovered that running faster on the hamster wheel only makes you better at ... well ... running on a hamster wheel. That wheel is called productivity and the cage is called progress. Get better at playing the game and you progress. But I would rather escape from the cage.

What I discovered was simple but profound: my job is to be happy, and this is my most important project, whatever I am doing at work today. And this happiness project is simple too; when I work with attention, awareness and mindfulness, I feel deep contentment right this moment. When I don't, I feel stressed, driven and future-focused. The stress tells me that I have forgotten my main project, and I am lost in some imagined future outcome.

Having realised this, I do what is needed to keep up with my work, but I don't seek the productivity badge of honour for most tasks done in a day, I care more about quality. I want to do every single thing with care, attention and presence, as if it were the most important thing in the world. Curiously, when I work in this way, I seem to figure out better things to work on, I have creative ideas and others seem to support my efforts. There is very little ego in this way of working, it's all focused on doing a better job, which is the opposite of the productivity cult.

Janet works for herself. She feels good when she gets things done, and she isn't fussed if things get better or not. She wants to feel useful, so she does. I want to make things better, so I go slow, I watch, I reflect, I take the time to ask why, and things keep getting better.

The universe, apparently, has taken billions of years to evolve to this point through a process of trial and error, of ongoing experiments, and humans are no different. The ego wants a quick win, a massive result this month and a promotion. Your true self wants to be fully engaged, and time has no meaning, so *how* you work now is all that matters.

So let's take a day to question not how to get things done faster, but what things we should do and how we should do them. What is your underlying energy as you work: stress or peace? And if peace was the driving feeling behind everything you do at work, what difference would this make to what you do and how you do it?

### Activity – Start With Peace

Take a moment to close your eyes and breathe. Go inside yourself and feel yourself breathing. Sink into this peace and allow your thoughts to move to the background.

Now take a moment to imagine yourself doing your work with this underlying sense of calm. How would you enter your workplace? What would colleagues notice as you sit down for the day? And what would you do differently through the course of the day?

Take a few minutes to picture this way of being at work, then try it out in the real world, next time you are at work.

True productivity is about contribution, and the primary thing that we each bring into the world is our energy. This isn't new-age wisdom or spiritual advice, it is an observable fact. When those around you are nervous, or stressed, or angry, that energy tends to spread. And if you are with someone calm, peaceful and happy, that is contagious too.

In my work life, my colleagues and teammates rarely get sick or take stress leave. Teams I am in always seem to function well, even when they involve people who don't get along that well outside of work. And the people I meet on a daily basis often comment that they leave feeling calm, content and peaceful. This is my true contribution to the world.

In this way, work is not a means to an end. Instead, it is a place to express the peace I feel inside, a way to bring this into the world. The things I seem to accomplish in the external world don't last, they come and go, but that peace seems to linger, even after the external structures have disappeared. This is true productivity.

## Day 2: Blending Mission and Purpose

As we have already seen during this journey together, the primary purpose of your life (and your work) is to become deeply connected with this moment, to be mindful. This is your purpose in this instant, to be completely present right now.

This purpose doesn't depend on any external achievement, effort or success, and sometimes complete failure is a better path to discovering this presence than the trappings of apparent success. Let's call it 'true purpose' for a moment.

True purpose doesn't exist as an achievement over time, something you work at, think about and chip away at it; it arises in this very instant, or it doesn't arise at all. Are you awake as you read this, alert to your surroundings, or are you lost in your mind? Is that voice absorbing your attention or is there some left to take in your surroundings?

If you sense that you are aware of your surroundings, attentive to your body and mind as they are right now, then you are fulfilling your true purpose. In a moment, you might forget that purpose again, as it's a moment by moment practice, but for now, you're here, congratulations!

As you work on a day-to-day basis, remembering your true purpose is very enjoyable and beneficial. It helps you to stay focused, to roll with the punches of daily work. On top of this true purpose, it is possible to have a sense of mission, of things you are driven to achieve in the external world, without losing yourself in mind once again. Today is all about balancing and blending the seemingly contradictory energies of present moment awareness and worldly achievement, which is the true art of living.

But mission, as I describe it here, isn't your five-year plan or your aims for the year, it runs a little deeper. Mission is what you know to do, what feels right for you to be engaged in at this time of your life. It has nothing to do with getting paid more, gaining social status or working towards some future image in your mind. All of these are common in that they start with a thought in your head, which is translated into a set of desires and a plan. Mission starts in the body, it *feels* like the right direction, even when it's scary, or it seems crazy or makes no sense. Even when you have no idea where it is taking you or why, you just know that you have no choice.

So mission starts in the body, and the mind gives it some structure, a path forward in the form of thoughts. But with mission as I define it, those thoughts are flexible, they evolve and change as the journey progresses, but that inner sense of direction remains. In your own work life, are you following a plan, or living according to mission?

## Activity – Finding Your Mission

In one sense, we are all in line with our mission, or in other words, we're in the right place for us right now. The whole universe conspired to put you there, so unless it made a mistake, you're where you should be.

And yet, if you take the time to tune into your inner self more clearly, you may find yourself moving in another direction, or continuing with more clarity. Here is a simple way to do this:

Take a moment to breathe and reflect on your work life. Close your eyes and remember the standout moments of your daily work. What inspires you, what makes you feel like you are in the right place? If there was one part of your job, or one way of doing your job, that you would like to do more often, what would it be?

To truly embrace this process of introspection, you will need to disregard the stories your mind tells about your job and your colleagues for a moment.

When, in your work, do you feel most alive? What are the common threads in terms of what seems to *feel* right in your work situation?

Sit with these questions for a few minutes, then allow the insights to bubble up over the next few days and notice what you discover.

This might seem a little ethereal initially, but if you continue to pay attention at work, you will start to notice that there are common threads that make you feel a sense of purpose and aliveness. Combine these with the practice of working with mindfulness and any job, regardless of its value in our culture, can become a mission that changes the world for those you come into contact with every day. In fact, working in this way is the only true achievement.

## Day 3: Balanced Relationships at Work

Our relationships as humans are upside down; they're focused on others, but they are all about us! Watch yourself and you will see how your mind wants to watch others closely and decipher what they think of you. Does she like you? Did they agree with what you said? Am I funny? This is where the mind is at home, lost out in the apparent world, thinking about what it all means.

And while this external focus may seem selfless, it's completely egotistical. When we fall into this trap, we're totally absorbed in what we think others think of us, and this matters because we are interested in improving our self-image. Of course, this isn't a conscious thing, it is a habitual pattern that we get drawn into. We're taught from an early age that the opinions of others matter, and we reinforce to children that they should behave in such a way that other people will approve.

For many, this conditioning leads to an unwitting existence, in which they try to find happiness by getting recognition in the outside world. In a way, then, we are using others to try to complete ourselves (or at least the image we have of ourselves); other people are just props in the show we are broadcasting!

At work, if you ever attend meetings, you will see this happening all over the place: people using big words that mean nothing, managers posturing and deflecting responsibility, and a stiff, bureaucratic air to the interactions between people who are quite normal outside of meetings! Sometimes this is extended to the game we call 'office politics', in which the winner is the craftiest, the one who deflects the most criticism and garners the best perks by manoeuvring their way through the organisation with the most skill.

How exhausting and destructive all these games are! And what a waste of human talent and creativity when we get lost in this quest to strengthen our sense of identity through our interactions with others. Being outwardly focused makes us selfish, because that whole game is aimed at making our self-image stronger.

So what is the alternative? How can you move beyond this childish quest for approval and find your own approval right now? Actually, it's quite easy. When you move your focus within, and drop the search for outer approval, that self-image is no longer so important, and in that state, helping others becomes as natural as breathing.

When I walk into work each day, I don't seek approval. In fact, I often have no idea whether people approve of me or not, it simply doesn't occur to me. And it's not that I am self-absorbed, quite the opposite in fact.

Sitting with my friend Anne, I get totally absorbed in what she says. I still notice my breathing and my body as I listen, but all thought seems to melt away. Listening in this way, I have no opinions about what she says or who she is, I just listen. And sometimes an idea comes into my mind, a thought that takes the conversation to a different place. I don't plan what I will say and I don't really care if it works or not, I just say it. Even as the words come out, I don't know what they will be, and after they come, I can't say that they were my great idea, they just occurred to me. I don't care a bit what Anne thinks of me, and so I can lose myself in the conversation, or lose the image of myself anyway. And without that self-image to protect and enhance, I am totally there for Anne, totally present. Inner-focused = selfless.

## Activity – Balanced Focus

For your focus to be in balance like this, you need to start inside and work your way out; start with inner focus and then notice your surroundings.

Close your eyes and feel your physical body. Notice how it feels to be standing, sitting or lying, notice how your clothes feel on your skin and sense the temperature of the air just by paying attention to your body.

Now, open your eyes and look around. Stay connected to your body and look with openness, mindfulness. If your mind comments on what you see, let it, but keep bringing attention to your body.

Notice how, when you aren't lost in thought, it's hard to know who it is that's looking. There's no clear sense of you as a particular person, there is just awareness of the world around you. You will still remember your name, I'm sure, and you won't lose the ability to live practically in the world, but the story of me, which probably takes up most of your attention most of the time, can move to the background for a moment.

Who are you when you're not thinking about your story? When you just look, who is looking? Awareness is looking. Welcome to reality.

A balanced relationship is one in which there is space, attention and awareness between you and the other. You are there as awareness, not as a needy little person with a hidden agenda. And without that agenda, you can be there in whatever way the other person needs right now, you can be the bringer of peace into the world around you.

Today, see if you can listen more than you talk, see if you can notice more than you judge, and start with your own awareness before you bring your opinions into the world. Try this shift, and see what sort of life it brings you each day.

## Day 4: Balanced Achievements

Many people I hear from are worried about being mindful (or their minds are anyway). They are worried that, if they become totally present, they will lose the ability to achieve or strive for goals, and in some ways they are correct, though not in the way you might think. Goals and mindfulness can co-exist, but not in the usual way.

Goals, in reality, are often more of a burden than a help for humans, assuming that happiness is your most important goal! What people usually call goals I would label as desires: things you think you need in order to be happy. And as I have written many times before, the belief that there is something you need before you can be at peace is the biggest barrier to experiencing peace right now.

Such goals, which I sometimes call 'stress goals', create tension in your life. There is often a sense of hope and energy when you imagine the goal being achieved, and lurking underneath this is the secret fear that you won't be successful.

And whether you are imagining success or failure, you are imagining, thinking about an imagined future, instead of living here and now. Living here and now is the only true success.

Because stress goals are reliant on an image of the future, they exist primarily in the mind as an outcome, a point you will reach if everything works out. True goals, however, which co-exist perfectly with a life of mindfulness, have a very different quality.

True goals involve living in alignment with your true self, which means that they are process goals, rather than outcome goals. A true goal is like setting your course for the west, and then with each step aiming to live *this* step well and then *this* step well. We usually say *the next step,* but if you look closely, it's always *this* step. Every step is an end in itself; the journey to the west is not a striving towards a destination, it is just one step.

For example, my true goal is to change as many people's lives as I can by bringing peace and mindfulness into the world. As I sit here writing, I am taking a step, but I'm not in a hurry. I'm not trying to get this book published quickly so I can achieve my goal. My goal will never be achieved, it will continue for as long as I do. And now I'm taking *this* step.

When I finish writing for tonight and I walk to the kitchen, this goal remains. I will walk with as much attention as I can muster, and I will talk to my wife with peace in my heart, as best I can. And whether this book gets finished or whether anyone reads it (I guess you can say yes to both), I am living in alignment with my true goal.

Living in this way, achievement stops being an ego thing. When people write to say that my books changed their lives,

I know it's not true. *They* changed their lives, and my words helped in the process. The way I see it, the universe wanted a book like that written, and it came through me. If I wasn't interested, someone else would have done the job.

This type of achievement is much more a shared celebration than the achievement of stress goals, which often involve beating someone else. True goals bring us closer together and true achievement is always shared. What are your true goals?

### Activity – My True Goals

It's likely that you have plenty of stress goals in your life. I did too, although most of them have dissolved by now. But what are your true goals? What purpose do you want your existence to serve? And how would you like to live each day in accordance with those goals?

Take a piece of paper and complete the following sentence:

*I want my life to bring* _____ *into the world.*
*In accordance with this I want to* _____
*every day.*

Now step into true goals for a moment. Take attention into your body and allow those true goals to sit with you in this moment. Feel yourself breathing, listen to your surroundings and be still with your purpose.

If you can't answer these questions, let them sit with you too. Allow that uncertainty to penetrate, don't try to avoid or escape it. If you sit in that uncertainty for long enough, answers will arise and you will find clarity.

True goals don't need to seem grand and they may change over time. Their underlying character, though, is that they represent a way of living as much as they speak of a destination. Ends and means are one.

Also, your true goals and your current job may or may not seem connected. But if you assume that you are in the right place for you right now, and then look for ways to express your true goals within your current work, you will be surprised to discover that the type of work you do matters much less than the way you do it.

## Day 5: Sitting in Conflict

When conflict arises in our lives, most of us have our own way of dealing with it, honed through years of watching others and practising. Our aim in doing this, usually, is to either eliminate the conflict, by escaping it or squashing it, or to reduce its impact by ignoring it or controlling our thoughts and feelings about it.

These approaches may have worked well or poorly (or a mix of both), but regardless of their apparent success, they reduce your ability to learn from, and grow through, these conflicts. Friction, after all, can create sparks that light new fires in your life, if you know how to work with it.

Today we will explore how you can learn to sit still in the midst of conflict, a skill that leads to some wonderful outcomes on an inner (and often an outer) level. And while powerful, this skill is as simple as learning how to be active in doing nothing.

This seeming paradox might put your mind in a spin, and that's fine. I will spell it out in a simple way that you will be able to start using in your life right away, but let's resolve the paradox first.

Being skilful in conflict means doing less, from an outside perspective. You will need to speak less, think less and act less. You will need to become comfortable appearing to do nothing. In reality, though, you will be listening more, noticing more and being more still, all of which requires some effort in the beginning. From an external perspective, you might look passive, but you will find yourself focused, alert, aware and attentive, and these qualities have the power to transform your inner experience, as well as the response of those around you.

## Activity – Stillness in Conflict

The next time you find yourself involved (directly or indirectly) in a conflict situation, try this simple process:

- Take a mindful breath to make you focused and alert.
- As you breathe, listen very carefully to what others say, without trying to think of your next statement. Just listen.
- Watch carefully, taking in what you see happening around you. Again, don't judge, just watch.
- If words come, let them come. If they don't, stay alert and still. If you are asked a direct question, answer it, then return to alertness as soon as you have done so.
- Once you have left the situation or it has finished, leave it alone, unless there is some practical action you can take to improve things right now.

If we assume that your inner peace is the most important thing (which is the way I like to approach life), then finding peace in the midst of conflict is a wonderful super power.

In conflict situations, the people involved are usually so lost in their own thoughts that they are unable to notice their surroundings or tune into the present moment. They are drowning in mind, and having someone present who is truly present (not just 'there') can be responded to in a couple of ways, both of which are good. First, they might throw you out, ask you to leave or attack you, and so (hopefully) you get to escape peacefully. Second, they might wake up out of thought a little themselves. It is hard to stay mind-identified when you are with someone who is mindfully aware, so people tend to either try to get you to identify with their thoughts too, or those thoughts loosen up a bit.

This can be a wonderful gift for those around you, but whether they respond well to your alertness or feel threatened by it, you get to deepen your experience of peace, even in the midst of turmoil. And this is a very nice thing to experience.

When conflict arises at your workplace, start to pay attention to your natural response. Are you habitually drawn into mind? Do you get hooked on the conflict? Or do you feel a strong urge to escape? Use mindfulness of your own thoughts and feelings to learn more about those habits and to increase your awareness of your experience in those moments.

Take this a little deeper and see if you can stay still in the midst of conflict, responding only when necessary and letting the issues resolve themselves or not. This frees you from taking a fixing role in the conflict and allows you to be there for yourself instead.

Even if that stillness is only there for a few seconds and

you are quickly drawn into old habits, you are making a start. Stick with this practice during difficult times and you will see old patterns start to lose their power, allowing you to take a constructive role in times of turmoil, while all the while deepening your inner stillness. What a wonderful gift these difficulties can be.

## Day 6: Growing Slowly

Everyone around me, it seems, is in a hurry. They need that report today, they need those stats yesterday and they need the new plan done by tomorrow. Why? Nobody knows, but once a date is set, it needs to be met!

'I hope to have it done by Christmas,' I hear them say, as if getting 'there' will bring some major change to their lives. Lao Tzu said:

'Others are excited,
as if they were at a parade.
I alone don't care ...'

And I know what he meant. Others rush around me, trying to achieve, to get and to become. I don't care about any of that. All I care about is this now. Sometimes my mind is interested in other things and sometimes I get lost in those ideas, but in my true self, there is no need for anything more.

I have nothing that I'm working on, nothing you would call a goal that is a step towards something. I'm writing this and spreading mindfulness as best I can, but that's not a goal, for me it's like breathing, it happens naturally, it's not my conscious plan to do it.

But in spite of this, I seem to keep growing and changing. Conventional wisdom would say that without a desire for a better future, someone like me should stagnate, trapped in the current state without any forward movement. This idea is flawed when you look around, though, and see that everything in the world developed according to its nature without needing a plan. Seeds become trees that grow flowers and fruit. Animals evolve, the universe expands, all without a single thought. Only humans believe they need the mind to move forward.

So what if you are growing, developing and learning not *because of* your mind but *in spite of it*? What if the path you are on as a person is only impeded by thinking so much and planning each step? This is what I discovered when I started to wake up out of thought.

It turned out that all the thinking, planning and analysis was overdone in my life. Every step was carefully planned and there was always an expectation of where it would lead. If it did not, stress arose, and if it did work out as planned, then I quickly refocused on the *next* step forward. Never was there a moment of contentment, of satisfaction; well, perhaps a moment, but no more than that, there was always more to achieve.

But as thought has receded to the background of my life, a process that continues today, I discovered that I never had a shortage of plans or ideas, I had a shortage of energy and awareness. I was spending so much energy on those plans that I had very little left to act, and I was so lost in those plans that I lacked awareness of what I was actually doing each moment.

As this awareness and energy have increased, something strange has started to happen in my life. Things I do in the outer world seem to become successful, and I keep growing and learning, improving everyday. This is because I stopped treating myself like a factory and turned myself into a garden instead.

## Activity – The Garden of You

Mostly people act as if their development were a manufacturing process – put yourself through a fixed set of processes and you will get a predictable result. Today I want to encourage you to start treating yourself like a garden instead.

When we nurture a garden, there is a strong element of mystery. We can plant certain things, but we never really know how they will develop, what shape they will take or how large they will grow. So instead of focusing on the result, we focus on creating the conditions for growth, and with mindfulness, you can do this for yourself at work too.

Plants need water, sunlight, nutrients and room to grow. We need awareness, mindfulness and space.

To create these conditions, you can simply shift your attention from thinking to being. Close your eyes and pay attention to what is happening in your body right now. Feel every sensation, allowing it to be exactly as it is.

Feel yourself breathing. Follow the in and out flow of each breath, noticing how it feels and letting it be just as it is right now. Let thoughts come and go, but don't get lost in them if you can help it. If you do get lost, come back to your breath.

Allow everything about you to be exactly as it is right now. Be curious about how it is, not sure about how it should be. Sit as you are in this instant, and allow the next change to happen naturally, in its own time.

Gardens don't grow in a hurry, they do everything at just the right time in response to their own cycle and the conditions around them. There is no hurry for you either. You are exactly as you should be right now, unless the universe made a mistake! So be watchful for your mind's projections and ideas about how you should develop and in what timeframe. Whenever that urge to rush to some better place arises, simply notice it, and allow your attention to move back to this instant, trusting yourself to grow at the rate you are supposed to, perfectly imperfect, right here and now.

## Day 7: Resting in the Gaps

Everyone I meet tells me they are busy. They run from one thing to the other from 9–5, filling up the day with appointment and tasks, all the while feeling overwhelmed and time poor. Time poor? Actually, we are drowning in activity. There is no time, so you can't be lacking it!

And yet, my friend Jamie swears that he is. Jamie has a full calendar almost every day, and he is often seen running down a hallway somewhere, on the way from something to something else. His favourite phrases through the day are" 'I'm going to have to head to my next meeting sorry' and 'I'm sorry for being late. My last meeting ran overtime.'

Jamie blames the outside world for his calendar problems. He claims that others demand too much, that his job is too big, that there is too much to get done. The truth, though, is that Jamie feels uncomfortable in spaces. He fills silence, he fills weekends, he feels anxious when he is not on the way somewhere because he is left alone with his mind.

Many people are like this, it seems, appearing to run from one thing to another, but actually running from their thoughts! Maybe you feel like this too, at least some of the time, and I'm sure you have at least one friend like Jamie. It's nothing personal, actually, it's simply the human mind in action, looking for something else, looking for more.

This is the 'normal' way of living, seeking happiness by adding more to your life and to your self. The mindful way is the opposite, continually dropping things you were seeking, things you were attached to. One method for finding a peaceful daily existence is to balance your activity by embracing space, stillness and silence.

There is no need to do anything special to create space and silence in your day, it is there already, you simply need to embrace it. Every one of us has opportunities to sit quietly, to do nothing, to be still, but often we try to escape them. And one of the best opportunities is the one we like the least; waiting.

Waiting is almost universally reviled in human society. Just the mere mention of it elicits sympathy, as in:

'I'm just waiting for the doctor'

'Oh, I hope you get in soon.'

But what if you could make waiting your friend? What if you could turn every inconvenient moment of waiting into a pleasure, a blessed relief? You can.

This change is big, but it's incredibly simple, as easy as a change of attitude. What was your response the last time you had to wait for something? Did you fret, feel impatient, upset, annoyed? If so, you were treating waiting as an obstacle, an enemy.

This is how most people treat delays, but there is another way: we can treat them as friends.

## Activity – Learning to wait

Try the following activity the next time you have to wait for something:

- Move your attention to your breath and notice how it feels to breathe in and out. Notice how your chest feels as it expands and contracts, feel your shoulders moving up and down, and smile.
- Sink into your chair if you are sitting, or feel your feet connect with the ground if you are standing. Become curious about how it feels to be you right now. Forget about where you think you are trying to get to, and just be yourself right now. What is that like?
- Keep coming back to this moment, using your breath as an anchor, and allow this delay to become your daily meditation. Thank goodness you got to stop a while, and return to your own self.

Actually, the only life worth living is this one, right now. The future you are trying to get to won't be better than this, it won't bring fulfilment, because it is no more than a thought in your head. And even if it comes true, it won't bring peace, your mind will just start chasing the next thing.

This sits at the heart of our human dysfunction; we are looking to the future and hoping that some addition to our lives will bring happiness. It's all here for us now, and learning to wait can bring us to this realisation.

So whether you are waiting for a promotion, waiting for an email or just waiting for your computer to load in the morning, you have a wonderful opportunity to embrace a different way of living. Do you want to live always seeking something else, or experiencing your life as it happens now? The choice is yours.

# WEEK 5

## Work as Your Mission

So far on our journey together, we have explored some simple ways to bring mindfulness into your everyday work life. These simple tools can make a big difference to your quality of life and can open up new ways of seeing yourself and the world. And this week, as our journey continues, you will discover the surprising power of making your work a way to clarify and fulfil your mission, even if your job is seen as menial by others (or yourself).

The word mission might seem grand, but to me it simply means the contribution you wish to make to the world. We all have something unique that we like to bring to our interactions with others, to our daily activities and to our lives outside of work. This week we will clarify what your contribution is and how to enhance it with a little mindfulness. The activities are designed to bring more attention and awareness to your work, as well as helping to make it clear what you most want to give to those around you.

If these contributions don't jump out at you, be patient and stay present, they will come when they are ready. And most of all, enjoy the process of taking attention inside and looking into your inner experience. It is the most rewarding thing you could possibly do.

## Day 1: Everyday Action

So far on this journey, I have emphasised the futility of keeping busy for the sake of it and the importance of choosing the right tasks and working with quality. Today I want to move in a slightly different direction by exploring the benefits of taking action every day when you have a clear sense of mission or purpose.

As we have explored in previous chapters, we need to start by bringing our attention into the present moment and finding the right direction for us now. Once that direction is clear, taking a step every day is a wonderful mindfulness practice and a great way to improve your work, as you will discover.

It appears that, apart from busy work, humans aren't so keen to take action. We love to plan, to strategise and to think about the future, but taking steady, regular action is not something we like so much. Taking such action can feel scary, risky, or even boring because the action that makes a difference is often steady effort over time, which is not so sexy to the mind.

Doing my own work, which is to sit here and write these words, is a good example. The idea of writing a book sounds quite interesting to most people, and many people ask me how I do it. But when I tell them to just write 1000 words every night forever, they give me a blank look or chuckle uncomfortably. It sounds too mundane, perhaps, to just sit at the keys and wait for 1000 words to come each night, but doing so is a step in the direction I am drawn to, which is to keep sharing what I have learned with those who wish to learn it too.

In Zen monasteries in Japan, there is a strong emphasis on this type of practice. There is a strong sense of routine and a great deal of everyday, seemingly mundane work to do, as well as lots of meditation. But there should be awareness, concentration and mindfulness in everything those monks and nuns do, and so this regular daily work is a crucial part of the practice.

For us too, work can be like a mindfulness retreat every day, if we know how to take action in the right way without delay.

### Activity – Finding Direction, Taking Action

Take a pen and a piece of paper and complete the following sentences:

*The contribution I want to make through my work is . . .*

*On my best day at work I would . . .*

Close your eyes for a moment and sit still with these answers. Allow them to wash over you, stay present and see what arises within.

Now take your pen in hand again and finish the following:

*To make that contribution stronger I could . . .*

*In this spirit, every day I would like to . . .* (Write four possibilities.)

Sit back once more and take in the answers on your page. Consider which one of these four possibilities you would like to make a daily practice in your work. For the next four days, commit to doing what you have chosen. Here is my own example to clarify what I mean:

*The contribution I want to make through my work is to show as many people as possible how to be peaceful.*

*On my best day at work I would find time for my own mindfulness practice.*

*To make this contribution stronger I could create something to share every day.*

*In this spirit, every day I would like to practise mindfulness, create something to share, sit quietly with a loved one, drink my tea in silence and go for a mindful walk.*

As you can see, I now have a blueprint for my daily work, and I hope you do too.

It might seem strange for the mindfulness teacher to put practising on the improvement list, but although I am often in the moment throughout the day, I don't always sit formally each day. My mind has many reasons for this, but all are mere stories, and maybe you have reasons too why your actions aren't possible, but try them out anyway.

In truth, it's unlikely that you *can't* do what you have written, though you might not always succeed. But clearly committing to taking action in this direction each day is a wonderful way to bring the avoidance tactics of the mind into clear focus.

As you take the action you have committed to, bring awareness, attention and presence into what you do. Be there totally as you act, and that attention will flow into what you do, improving the quality as well as your enjoyment. Then, forget about the quality, don't assess yourself or judge your performance. Just do it, over and over again with careful attention and trust that you will improve over time. People don't fail because they aren't good enough, they fail because they don't keep going long enough to get good at what they are doing.

And this is the secret, of mindfulness and of life. Practise in quantity, with as much quality as you can, but without the perfectionistic tendency to quit while you are still learning the basics. Make taking action in your true direction a daily practice and it will find its own rhythm quite naturally as you continue to execute.

This type of attitude can make any job into a calling and any calling into a powerful contribution to yourself and to the world. What will you do today?

## Day 2: Knowing the Course

There is a caution that it would be wise to apply to yesterday's work. Finding direction is vital, and committing to action in that direction at work every day is immensely rewarding. But sometimes, the mind can take over this process and turn direction into stubbornness, rigidity, inflexibility. Sometimes, when thinking takes over, this can become the path of the extremist rather than a fluid, flowing contribution to this wonderful world.

So today, we will explore how to maintain flexibility once we have established direction.

Many people seem to find a sense of their true direction penetrating through the layers of thinking and mind activity that takes up most of their attention. Through this fog, a few rays of sunshine make it to their consciousness, and they discover a feeling of what they want to do with their lives.

But as people fall back into that mind activity, the direction can quickly be hijacked by the mind. For example, if you discover great joy in creating and making music, and realise that you want to do more of that, your mind may sneak in, telling you either about the fame and wealth you can accumulate by getting good enough, or about the imminent failure of your endeavours because you will never be good enough! When I write books I notice that my mind wants to fantasise about how many copies might sell or how much I might earn, and when I get lost in these thought streams, the work loses its joy and it feels stressful.

The heart of this dysfunction is the mind's tendency to take something you enjoy now, project it into the future and evaluate whether it is worth doing now. That evaluation is based on how continuing may affect the future, while true joy arises when you do what feels right now without trying to get something from it.

And when the future outcome (which is imagined) takes over, then doing that work starts to feel heavy, burdensome and lifeless. The results of each action become more important than the experience of acting, and the end point of the action seems fixed. In this frame of mind, it is very difficult to see unexpected opportunities, to change course or to re-evaluate once you have started. All of these seem like failure to the mind.

In our musical example before, you might discover, after years of playing around with music, that you have a knack for using music to help people with learning difficulties, or that you want to become a music therapist. Or you might just keep enjoying playing. But these results are only possible if you can sidestep the mind's tendency to get fixated on a particular result.

Doing this is actually surprisingly simple, but it does require a high degree of alertness and awareness, a continual stepping back into the present moment. In fact, all that is needed is to disregard that future projection, and to keep coming back to the task at hand right now, to doing your daily work. Make doing the work and paying attention as you do your only concern, and simply allow those thoughts about where it might lead to come and go without getting lost in them.

## Activity – Noticing the Future

For many people, work revolves around this hoped for future. They start with that vision and work their way back to the logical steps to take now. In mindfulness we do the opposite, we start with the work that seems important now, and we do that work well. Once that work is done, we see what is needed next.

To clarify what is important, I sometimes ask myself what the present moment is asking of me right now. What is the world asking me to do? And as I ask this question, my mind starts to crowd in with visions of what I 'need' to happen in the future, and what I need to do now to create that.

These two approaches couldn't be more different. In one, I trust the world to give me direction, and I trust that this will lead to what is best for me. In the other, I feel I know best and I try to impose my ideas on the world, something that rarely works.

To discover which approach you are using at work, you can simply take a few minutes to close your eyes and watch your mind at work. Allow thoughts to come and go undisturbed, simply watching them and noticing what they are about.

As you watch, see if you can leave all future projections alone. Don't get drawn into mentally playing with them, crafting a more detailed picture of the future, just watch. See how the mind takes the contribution you want to make now, the work you want to do now, and turns it into a projected future.

This insight, this noticing, is very powerful. It enables you to leave the future alone and do your best work today instead, to let tomorrow sort itself out. Working in this way, you stay fresh, agile and flexible. You can quickly adapt to new opportunities and circumstances while continuing to contribute to the world around you. As a side effect, this approach also seems to lead to the career success that the mind craves, but only if you do the work for its own sake, without thinking about what you'll get out of it.

And as you bring this freshness, this aliveness to your important work, you bring something new into the world, an undercurrent of peace that is more valuable than anything you could achieve in the external world.

# Day 3: Mindful Service

Often when we think of the contribution we wish to make at work, it is framed in terms of activities and outcomes. And when we celebrate the work of important people in our society, we often focus on what they did, what they achieved, without noticing how they treated others or what impact they had on those around them.

Today I invite you to consider what you contribute at work beyond what you do. Instead, let's explore how your way of being affects those you come into contact with on a daily basis, and the ripple effect that may have in the universe. And finally, you will see how starting with your own peace and happiness allows this contribution to be amplified.

It might be pretty easy to measure what you do. You work at the bank, or the supermarket, or you lay concrete. This 'what' is the thing that your mind is probably interested in. We describe what we do when we say 'I'm a teacher/counsellor/nurse' and it is often what gives us a sense of identity, a story about who we think we are.

But what you do isn't significant when it comes to your contribution to the world; your true contribution comes from *how* you do what you do. And this 'how' isn't about technical skills or expertise in your job. It isn't even about your outer attitude as you work – it is all about your attention.

As you work, are you thinking, or are you working mindfully, are you present? Is your work a moment by moment experience of this instant, or is it a means to an end, a path to a better future? The answer to these questions will tell you where your attention is as you work, in the now or in thought; these are the only options.

Of course, your state of awareness probably fluctuates throughout the day, perhaps even minute by minute, but what if you made your attention priority number one? Doing so is easier than it may appear.

Just for this week, try this. Make your inner state the most important focus throughout your day, or to be more specific, bring mindfulness to your work day, as if you were not at work but on a retreat. Do your work as normal, but bring more attention, care and focus to it, and make this attention your only goal.

As your inner state settles, pay close attention to others, be mindful with them too. Listen wholeheartedly, look wholeheartedly, be there with your entire body as you work and as you spend time with colleagues and customers. Awareness is like an energy current flowing through you, and it is the primary thing you bring into this world when you are in a state of mindfulness. The energy of presence spreads.

If you have ever had contact with someone who works from this state, even if they don't dwell there in other parts of their life, you will know what I mean. Coming into contact with someone who is calm, alert, peaceful and content is contagious. Everything seems to settle down in their presence and when you leave, you bring that sense of calm into your next interaction. Peace is contagious and you are a carrier.

It is a universal law that energy is never created or destroyed, it simply moves, spreads and changes form. The energy of mindfulness is no different, and you can harness it to spread joy through your daily work. This may sound strange because you can't see it, but we can't see electricity or telephone signals, but we believe in them because we have seen their effects. Watch the impact of being mindful during your daily work and you will see that they are quite tangible and visible, even if awareness is not.

> ### Activity – Coming Back
>
> Most people will need regular reminders to return to this state of awareness throughout the day. To do this, try choosing an activity or a signal that happens several times each day. This could be the phone ringing, the chiming of a bell, or logging on to your computer, for example.
>
> Whenever that signal occurs or that activity is required, take two or three mindful breaths (which will take only a few seconds) and then continue with the energy of mindfulness.
>
> Doing this many times throughout the day is a powerful way to start to integrate mindful work into your regular day. Try it this week and you will see how much more enjoyable work is when you are here to do it, rather than being somewhere else mentally.

As an experiment this week, try shifting your main aims from being about what you do to being about the energy you bring. Make mindfulness your primary goal at work and let everything else flow from that. Then, see how it feels for you and how others respond to this approach. The results of such a subtle shift may be faster and more powerful than you would have imagined.

# Day 4: The End of Improvement

There is a sure-fire way to get better: stop trying to improve! This is a heretical statement, because everybody knows that the path to improvement is to identify weakness, set goals and make plans. And everybody is wrong.

In your work, there are always opportunities to get better, of course. But there is a curious paradox that operates when it comes to improvement, which is that you have to stop chasing it in order to find it. That is what today is all about.

A giant leap happened this week in my mindfulness practice. I went from being in and out of thought to a near constant state of ease and awareness, and the way this occurred is curious: I stopped trying to get better.

When you are trying to improve, there is a natural tendency to look outside, to observe or listen to others and copy their moves, to do some training or to practise harder. This can work, but it has an inbuilt limitation, which is that it tends to draw attention outside yourself. You think about what others have said, evaluate yourself against their results and keep trying to emulate them.

Far more effective than this, though, is to pay attention to what you are doing now, to love and appreciate it, even. In this, there is a chance to truly grow.

And as I continued my practice this week, sitting, practising some techniques and listening to some of my favourite teachers, I was following this old model. And then I stopped. I stopped trying to get better, to stay focused, to be alert. I forgot about techniques and quotes and just observed myself, and then I noticed something. I noticed that, in every practice I do, the first few seconds are the sharpest. The first mindful breath, the first move into the body, the first moment of listening. After that, attention starts to taper, and it takes real effort to return to awareness. And so the idea arose to only practise for one breath. So that's what I'm doing (I'm calling them 'one breath wonders'), just feeling one breath, then going on with normal activity, and the difference is tremendous.

But the process is of more interest than the result. If you drop your attempts to improve your work and watch it closely instead, two things will happen. First, the energy of allowfulness, of letting this moment be just as it is while simultaneously looking to improve things, will enter. This is the spirit of being content with what is and curious about how it could be better, all at the same time. And second, your attention will start to move from thinking to experience, to life as it is happening now.

This second effect is what leads to rapid improvement, to leaps and breakthroughs. Thinking can't achieve these because it is a sort of regurgitation of what you already know. Experience, however, is happening now. It's fresh and new and if you study it, something may occur to you that never came to you before.

But all of this is, of course, secondary. Stop thinking about improvement and the biggest gift is that you begin to appreciate your life at work. As you stop judging, you make friends with your work, you become curious about it and there is energy, enthusiasm and peace there, all at once. But how is it possible to discover this spirit and work in this way? As usual, it's easy than it first appears.

## Activity – Watch

When you go to work today, I invite you to bring a different sort of energy to your work – the energy of curiosity.

Most people think all day long, about what they need to do, about what should be different and about whether they like or dislike things, people and events. How tedious! Instead, today, bring the spirit of exploration, of noticing and watch closely.

Start by noticing what you see as you walk into work. Look at the colours, the shapes, the sights you can see, and pay careful attention to those sights. Look as if you had never seen those things before, and keep shifting from thinking to directly experiencing the world, as often as you can.

Watch with appreciative eyes, smiling and breathing as you observe what you see as you work. Don't try to dissect and analyse what is happening, but stay curious. Wonder why things are a certain way, and how they could be improved, without jumping to a particular answer.

And above all, stay alert, present and aware, and let any possible improvements come to you by themselves.

Enjoy your work first, allow it to be as it is, then as you notice with more and more alertness, you will see how you can do better. The seeing itself will show you the way, without the need for outside help, or help from your thinking mind. And adjustments will happen without so much effort, struggle and striving, because once you see clearly, there is no going back.

Play with this approach over the next few days and see how your experience at work changes, as well as the insights that come as an added bonus.

# Day 5: The Importance of Difficulty

This week we have been exploring the practice of treating your work as your mission, as your contribution to the world. And no mission can meaningfully proceed without some difficulties cropping up along the way. Indeed, it is these challenges, and the way we deal with these challenges, that enable the deepening of our present moment awareness. These hardships, be they unfairness in the workplace, difficult colleagues or thankless, demanding work, can be harnessed as fuel for your happiness practice and turned into wonderful blessings. Today I will show you how you can dive head-first into those challenges and transform them into incredible gifts.

If you are anything like the rest of the human race, then chances are that things happen every day that you don't like. Maybe they seem cruel or unfair, maybe those around you are hypocritical, or maybe you don't have the resources you need to do the job you want. That's bad, right? Well, it depends.

It depends on your approach, your attitude towards what happens. It depends whether you resist or work with what life is giving you right now. Your approach changes everything.

Every day, all around the world, people pay others to make their lives harder. We employ personal trainers, coaches, counsellors and others to challenge us, to make us suffer temporarily. In spite of our socialisation to avoid difficulty and find the easy way, we pay good money to be made uncomfortable, to sweat and hurt (physically, emotionally or both) and to struggle. Why do we do this? We embrace these challenges because we know that there is growth to be found through them, that we will be stronger, faster, or more emotionally resilient after we go through those fires.

And yet, when challenges arise at work, we are not always so keen to endure them. We may tend to shirk those challenges, to delegate that work, or to put it off until the last moment. And the difference, I think, is in our perception of control.

The gym, for example, seems pretty controlled. We can stop if we want and (as long as we don't overdo it) we will not be harmed by what we experience. At work, there is an air of unpredictability when challenges arise. When you feel the need to speak up about a colleague's behaviour, or to question your organisation's direction, there is a risk to the ego that can't be predicted, controlled or managed. There is no blueprint to follow, and no guaranteed ten-point plan that will lead to success. It's life, and it's unpredictable.

Of course, life is entirely unpredictable, but we tell ourselves a different story. You could lose your job tomorrow, or get a promotion, or get hit by a bus. Literally anything could happen. But we like to pretend that there is some order to the universe and that what we think will happen will actually happen. So the unpredictability of workplace challenges can become a doorway to living from a position of not-knowing, of not trying to control the universe, but letting it be instead.

The Zen masters call this 'Beginner's Mind' and it is a position of great openness, curiosity and aliveness. It is also a very vulnerable, uncomfortable place for the human mind, which, by its nature, wants to know.

So today, I want to introduce a simple method of allowing challenges at work to break open your habitual thoughts and beliefs, allowing you to step into the curiosity and wonder of this instant.

## Activity – Losing Control

Close your eyes for a moment and bring to mind a challenge you are experiencing (or have experienced recently) at work. Notice how your body responds to the thought of this challenge.

Focus on your breath for a moment and allow that memory to be present with you right now. As you feel yourself breathing, notice how you can't even control that, you can't even guarantee the next breath. Notice how all you have is this breath.

Feel the chair underneath you, and notice how the ground under the chair supports you right now. Consider how many celestial bodies have to spin in the right way with the right momentum to create the gravity that holds you in place right now. Notice how you can't control that either.

Consider all the things you seem to have control over – your job, your car, your body – and ask yourself whether you actually control any of it. Can you keep your body healthy when it's not? Can you make your car go when it doesn't?

And finally, try to think of something, anything that you have complete control over. Can you find even one single thing?

Now come back to that workplace challenge. Imagine yourself embracing it wholeheartedly without the need to control the outcome. Picture yourself doing your best without trying to get any particular outcome and notice what that would be like.

This week, take stock of the challenges you would like to avoid. Go through the activity above and see how your relationship with them changes. Then, see if you can allow each difficulty to be a reminder to step fearlessly into the present moment. See if you can turn difficulty into your greatest teacher.

## Day 6: A Deeper You

When thinking dominates your life at work, much energy is wasted pondering what else could be. Maybe there's a better job out there. Maybe your manager could be nicer. Or maybe you should have stuck with that accounting course you started at university. And when we spend our time thinking about other things instead of paying attention to now, opportunities are missed. Work can take you to a deeper experience of yourself, it can give you more breadth as a person, but not if you are busy thinking.

A common concern people raise with me when we talk about living in the now is that they won't be able to think anymore, but the truth is a little different. Thought is a part of human experience, so even if you embrace mindful living, it won't disappear, but it will start to change. Normal thought, if you watch it, is repetitive, stressful and mostly useless. It gives you anxiety and worry and contributes very little because it arises primarily from fear. Fear of missing out, of failing, of losing or not gaining what your mind thinks you need, fear of the future being not quite right.

This type of thought has an anxious energy to it; you can feel your body resisting as it arises. Fear has a tendency to feel that way.

Mindful thought is deeper, slower and more powerful, and today is all about how to use the thoughts that come to deepen your experience of life, how to move from shallow to deep thought.

Shallow thought is a hamster wheel, and when Jodie is on it, I can almost see her eyeballs spin. She talks faster, her tone is anxious, angry and upset, and there is drama in her words. And as Jodie talks, I just listen, holding the space of mindfulness, of pure listening. In that space, things start to slow down, and her ideas deepen. I remind Jodie to come back to now, and she smiles.

Suddenly, Jodie can see other perspectives. Her body and mind start to settle and her speech slows. There are gaps now, and still I let her speak, knowing that the right answers are her own. And then, the insights start to flow. Jodie finds new options opening up, new ways to approach the situation from a place of peace and contentment. And not only has her ability to deal with this situation changed, she also has moved deeper into her own self, into this moment.

Deep thought isn't something you do, it's the clarity that emerges when you allow the mud to settle while continuing to direct attention towards the situation. This practice, of sitting with the problem without trying to think your way through it, is counterintuitive, countercultural, and it works.

### Activity – Deeper

Take a moment to watch what is happening in your mind right now, without trying to change it one little bit. Feel yourself breathing and watch what thoughts arise now, letting each thought come and go in its own time.

As you breathe and watch, be on the lookout for gaps in

between thoughts, for moments when silence is there without any thought arising. There's no need to hold on to these gaps, just experience them.

If thought tries to draw you into some struggle to figure things out, take a step back, return to your breath, feel your body and watch what arises.

Whatever types of thoughts are arising, let them be there. Allow your mind to settle in its own time, just stop stirring it by playing with the thoughts that arise. Leave it alone and let your mind do its work.

Spend a few minutes just breathing and watching, allowing your mind to refresh itself. Take some time each day to do this during your work day and see what happens to the quality of your thoughts. You will be surprised what a difference it makes to give your mind a little rest.

In many jobs, the hamster wheel approach is encouraged. Think quick, make a decision, do something and move on. That's fine for simple matters, but if it becomes your default way of thinking, then you will remain on the surface of yourself.

When you make deliberate time to slow down, allow thought to have a rest and embrace those little gaps that arise, you will start to notice some interesting things. Firstly, when you slow down, better ideas come, and they come often. When the mind is freed from the fearful, shallow thinking it is used to, then a deeper intelligence emerges.

Secondly, you will find that thinking becomes less important. It no longer holds all your attention, it is a background phenomenon. And as a support player, thinking is wonderfully helpful. It gives shape to ideas that can bring new things into the world, it helps us to solve problems and improve the world around us. It is a blessing.

At work this week, make it your practice to use these simple skills to deepen your thinking, or to allow it to deepen. If you give it the space to do so, you will be amazed at the peace, creativity and energy that emerges as soon as the hamster wheel slows down.

## Day 7: Learning How to Stop

Work might seem like a barrier to your mindfulness practice. After all, it takes up time, puts you in difficult situations and creates all sorts of dramas in your life. But work has much to teach you about living in mindfulness, and today we will explore how work can teach you to stop.

Sitting at my desk, I'm completely still. I'm not thinking about anything, not doing anything, I just am, and people think I'm strange.

'How can you have time to do nothing?' they ask. 'Shouldn't you be doing something?'

Actually, I'm doing something far more important than 'something', I'm doing nothing. In the *Tao Te Ching*, Lao Tzu wrote of the mindful person:

'The Master does nothing,
yet he leaves nothing undone.
The ordinary man is always doing things,
yet many more are left to be done.'

The Master, as Lao Tzu describes him or her, has learned how to do nothing, and this is how I try to approach my work. Doing nothing is deeper than it sounds and it has two distinct elements.

First of all, 'doing nothing' does not mean laziness, it means strategically stopping. On an outer level, this stopping is the key to gathering energy, resetting your system and preparing to act decisively and skilfully. Sports stars stop before the game, readying themselves for the contest. Musicians and artists pause before they begin, channeling their energy and skill into the performance. And you too can use the simple act of stopping for a minute or two to regather yourself, to centre and anchor your awareness, and to move forward again with enthusiasm and skill.

The second element of doing nothing is internal, and it speaks to Lao Tzu's true meaning. He didn't mean that the Master sits around and everything magically does itself. What he was pointing to was that the Master (and the mindful person) does not have an identity as she acts, there is just awareness of the task as it is done. The Master 'does nothing' because she is so totally present as she acts that there is no sense of 'I' in it.

This 'I' is only there when we are thinking. If there is a running commentary going on as you work, then there is a sense of: 'I've finished the lesson plan now, so I just need to get the science experiment organised and then I'll be all prepared.' There is someone doing all this, or there is an image in your mind of someone (me) doing all this. In reality, there is no separation between you and your work, it is part of you and you are part of it.

Of course, from the outside, you are still the one doing

the work, but when you work with mindfulness, there is such presence that there is no story about the work you are doing, no thinking going on, it just happens by itself.

So we can stop on two levels. Level one is to stop doing periodically and just be. Level two is to stop thinking, even as you are engaged in action. Both of these ways of being are extremely countercultural, as our society values doing and being busy, and encourages us to take ownership of what happens in our lives. But if we strike a balance between being and doing and if we learn to work without thinking, there is great power and peace in this way of living.

### Activity – Stop Twice

Today I have a revolutionary experiment for you to test, two actually. I will show you how to secretly build stopping into your day on the external and the internal level, regardless of what you do.

External stopping is as simple as taking thirty seconds to do absolutely nothing, two or three times a day. You can be standing, sitting or lying down, but you have to do *nothing*, no devices, no audio, no books, absolutely nothing.

To do this, just find a spot where you won't be interrupted for thirty seconds. You might have to hide somewhere, or pretend to studiously read an email for thirty seconds, or put on your headphones. This can even be done on your toilet break if you have a really rigid workplace culture!

Once you have the time and the place, close your eyes if you can, go inside yourself and notice what is happening in you. Watch the breath come and go, and be still. Don't worry about what happened or what's next, just be. And after your thirty seconds is up, go back to work and notice how you do your job for the next little while.

As you continue your work, play with the second level of stopping – the internal. See if you can be so focused on your work that you don't have room for a story about how well you're doing, how good (or bad) you are and what you have to do next. Just be there, doing the work with complete attention.

Notice how, when you are this engaged in activity, your sense of self fades to the background. For many, this happens when they are doing something they 'love', or something that is novel and new. In those situations, there can be such intensity or contentment in the activity that there is no story there. Attention is focused on doing, not thinking.

It may seem as if only certain activities, those you 'love' or those that seem exciting or interesting, are suitable for this level of concentration. But in fact, in everything we do we can choose to either be alert and mindful or we can be thinking about something else.

What you do isn't so important. What matters is how you do it, and whether you can remember how to stop.

# WEEK 6

## Working in Flow

On our journey together so far, we have explored mindfulness at work from several different angles, and I hope that, by now, you are finding ways to try parts of what we have covered.

As we move into the final week of this journey together, I would like to weave these elements together into a coherent whole. In reality, if you practise any one of the activities in this book regularly, you will find yourself dwelling in the present moment. All of the elements lead to the same place, and there is no need to master them all in order to experience peace.

But I suspect that it will be helpful to see how these elements fit together as we bring to a close our time together. I hope this last week provides clarity, insight and enthusiasm.

### Day 1: Do It Now!

The first element of mindful work is intense focus on the present moment. This means that we experience what happens rather than thinking about it. It means that we do what is needed without thinking about it. And it means that we walk away from each task, each day and each job without creating an identity out of it, no story, no problem.

For most people, work has the complete opposite function: it reinforces and builds their story of themselves. Work becomes a part of the identity that hardens around those stories, as we identify with the things that happen, the role we play and the status our society gives to that particular job. Notice how you introduce yourself at a dinner party. 'My name is Jill. I'm a nurse at the local hospital.' Notice how what you do becomes who you 'are'?

Inevitably, this leads to a lot of thinking, analysis of the past and future projection to make sure that the imagined self is protected. Even someone else having a different opinion or criticising your work then becomes a threat to that self, and so there is much defensiveness and fear in this approach. It also happens completely unconsciously.

But most importantly, this is the path to a work life of stress and suffering. Whenever your attention moves from experience to thought, and whenever you become completely absorbed in thought, you will suffer before too long. But what would it be like to work entirely in this very instant?

When I walk into work each day, I hardly know what day it is, but I never forget an appointment. I don't spend a moment worrying about what I have to do tomorrow, and I'm always prepared. And I never regret, worry about or feel angry about what happened yesterday, and I still learn and grow from each thing that I experience.

How can this be? How can disregarding everything our society encourages lead to such a successful, rewarding and peaceful experience at work? The answer is simple.

When your responses, actions and words arise from thought, they come from the past, as the mind is a recording device for past events. Those ideas are old, pre-prepared like ready-made meals, and they don't provide much nutrition. Life is happening now and your mind is regurgitating some old thought.

On top of this, those responses are driven by the emotions of fear and desire. Fear of losing or missing out and the desire to get something extra in order to be happy. This is the other side of the mind: it analyses the old and projects the perfect future, so fear and desire are inevitable companions in this state of being.

When you act out of your awareness and your direct experience, however, the response will be appropriate to the situation. In fact, we could say that what you do arises *with* the situation, is part of the situation, so naturally it matches what is needed.

Imagine a tennis player who thinks about what shot to play next, based on their previous experience and their knowledge of the correct shots to play in different situations. Their shots will not be a direct response to the state of the game, but a prearranged pattern based on logical thought. And they will be terrible.

Show the same player how to improvise in response to the state of the match and they will improve dramatically, and your work will too, if you allow yourself to be more instinctive.

The following is a simple practice for becoming present in the everyday tasks of your daily work.

## Activity – Now!

When you first walk into work in the morning, you may need to plan for the day and think ahead. Once this planning is done, you can shift attention continuously into the experience of working, right now.

You can start by moving attention from thought to what you can see right now. Become intensely aware of what images surround you, of what your world looks like in this instant.

Look with intensity, and allow what you see to be as it is. Bring curiosity rather than judgement and notice all of the different colours, shades and shapes that are in your field of vision.

See if you can feel the difference between really looking without analysing and being lost in thought. Notice how it feels to be here, now as the watcher of what is.

Now get up and move, and make awareness of those movements your main focus. Feel what it is like to stand, to sit, to walk. Feel the state of your body right now, notice how it is to dwell in this body.

And notice how you can still look around, how you can still move, act and even talk from this state of awareness.

Continue this practice for the rest of the day, look carefully and move with awareness. Don't try to achieve anything through it, just play with this way of being at work, and notice what it is like to be totally present, even for brief moments, as you work.

What you will discover as you practise this is that your mind lied to you. Thinking doesn't help you most of the time, it gets in the way. Being present isn't an obstacle, it is a powerful way of living. And there is no reason for continuing to create stress by acting as if the past and the future were more important than this.

## Day 2: Working With Purpose

Every day, as I work, I have two purposes. The first is to be mindful – this is my life's mission. That sounds a bit overwhelming, but luckily I only have to do it right now, tomorrow I can do something different (if it ever comes). My second purpose is to bring that mindfulness into action, to be present as I do things in this world.

The rest of what I do is secondary. I do it as well as I can, of course, but I have no attachment to it, and I could step out of my profession into something else without any regrets. When I am engaged in my daily work, I am totally committed to it and I love it. As soon as I leave, it is forgotten.

And during my work day, I structure my time, as much as I can, to meet these two purposes as well as I can, and I do this by working in a way that I like to call 'Stop and go'.

Most people work in a way that I would call 'Go go go!' and I'm sure that you are familiar with this method. What I do, instead, is to build small gaps into my day, during which I stop completely. These gaps range from about thirty seconds to about ten minutes.

During these gaps, I practise simple awareness activities, like mindful breathing, mindful walking or body awareness. And after those gaps, I continue with my normal work with as much awareness as I can muster. In practice, this makes my mornings look something like this:

9am: two minutes of breath awareness
9.02–10.30am: mindful work
10.30–10.40am: ten minute mindful walk
10.40–12pm: mindful work

It's quite incredible how much impact these twelve minutes of awareness practice have, and I really notice the difference between the days when I stop and those when I keep going. That stopping may seem like a luxury, but it has such an influence on the quality of my work for the rest of the day that I see it as an investment rather than a cost.

The other thing I do different to most people is that, rather than using mindfulness to be better at work, I treat work as my daily mindfulness practice. So when I step in the door, I have the same attitude as I would if I was going on a retreat. I see each step as an opportunity to connect more deeply with the present moment and I use the challenges that arise to help my practice to grow.

This subtle shift makes a dramatic difference to the way my days unfold, because it allows me to embrace everything that happens, and to deliberately make mindfulness a part of my day. I still have plenty of challenges, I still get lost in stories and I often drift away from the present, and so my practice continues. But treating work as a mindfulness retreat reduces the impact of these events, makes them a helpful part of the journey and brings me back to now, over and over again.

### Activity – Your Daily Retreat

Take a pen and paper now and write out your own daily retreat schedule. Take a few minutes to consider your typical work day and find three or four thirty-second to ten-minute intervals that you could use to practice mindfulness.

Once you have identified these, think about what practices you will use. Will you practice simple breath awareness or go for a mindful walk? Will you put some guided practices on your phone, or will you fly solo? Make a rough plan for your next work day, treating it like a mindfulness retreat.

On your next work day, put this plan into action as best you can. Take the opportunities you have to stop and be present, and then treat the rest of your day as a mindfulness retreat, acting with as much awareness as you can manage.

The most wonderful thing about treating work like a mindfulness retreat is that it does not interfere with your work, not one bit. In fact, you will find that your work will improve, your stress levels will plummet and you will become an invaluable member of your team (if you have one).

Working in this way, you can be fully concentrated on your work while being friendly, energetic, enthusiastic and calm. This combination is such fun, and it flows beyond yourself to those around you. Your career, your team, your organisation and the world all benefit when you bring awareness to what you do.

But don't take my word for it! Make your next day at work a mindfulness retreat and see what difference it makes. I promise that you will never go back.

# Day 3: Love Thy Co-Worker

It might sound a little bit strange, but I love the people I work with. I smile when I see them, I feel great affection towards them and I genuinely love them in a completely platonic way. There's no attraction or desire there, and I don't even need to be friends with them outside of work, but when we are together at work, I think they are the most wonderful people to spend time with.

Let me be clear, though, sometimes I don't *like* the way they act, sometimes they can be real pains! It's not that my workmates are special in any way. They are quite ordinary, everyday people with seeming faults, weaknesses and character flaws. Sometimes they're grumpy, sometimes they are angry, and sometimes we disagree.

When I look at them, though, if I look underneath all that conditioning, there is something wonderful and loveable. I see myself reflected back. I have looked deep into myself and found that underneath all stories, I am just awareness, just life living itself. And when I look past the conditioning of my workmates, I see the same: awareness, life, experiencing this world right now.

And when you look at others without stories, without calling them something, without analysing what they do, that clear-eyed looking itself is love. In fact, love is your natural state, and it is only the stories you believe about others that obscure that love.

So what we are talking about is not an emotional state or a belief based on shared experience, it is quite simply the act of being together without thinking, being together in awareness. You don't actually need to like the other person to do this. They might have heavy conditioning that makes them disagreeable, unkind and difficult, but if you can be with them without making a story out of these behaviours, you can be there with this pure awareness.

### Activity – Awareness

Take a moment to get in touch with this awareness right now. Close your eyes and feel yourself breathing, become aware of what breathing feels like right now.

As you feel your body breathing in and out, ask yourself who it is that is watching the breath. Who is it that notices all that is happening?

See if you can sense not just the breath, but also the watcher of the breath, the awareness that is there in the background.

Notice the thoughts that are passing through your mind right now. Watch them as they come and go. Can you see that there is thought happening and then there is someone who is aware of thought? Who is that?

Obviously, that someone is you. You are the awareness of all these things, not the things themselves.

Usually, for most people, that awareness (also known as you) continually identifies with things that happen within or without. We identify with beliefs, thoughts, physical attributes and material possessions, and then we begin to confuse those things with 'me'.

To identify means to make your relationship with that thing a part of your self-image. In relationship to co-workers, this often means that we identify with an opinion about them, or that we create a story about them and then think about how that story interacts with our self-image. For example, my self-image might include the notion that I am unappreciated at work. If I believe my boss is nasty, or that a certain customer is difficult, then the memories of me dealing with these people can be used by the mind to reinforce that belief, in turn strengthening my self-image.

And so, most relationships at work (and elsewhere) are driven by our fears and desires. We want something from others (recognition, approval, status, etc.) and we fear that they might take those things away from us. So people (to the mind) are either tools to get what we want or threats. It's no wonder relationships are so difficult!

Because of this way of being, most people never really meet anyone else, they only meet their own thoughts about those people. These stories act like a buffer between you and others, preventing true connection.

But if you can be with your colleagues and stay in touch with the awareness that is the background of your experience, then a different way of being together can arise. Without stories getting in the way, we can connect with our colleagues as they are right now, we can allow them to be as they are without trying to change them (although we can still point out things they are doing that create problems) and we can be there without wanting anything from them or fearing them.

This is revolutionary. You can be the one who accepts your colleagues as they are, the one who is there listening without pushing a particular agenda. Imagine working with a team of people who were always calm, peaceful and content. Imagine being accepted as you are and supported unconditionally by your teammates. This is the gift you can give every day to your team.

And the best part? To do it, you need to be present, peaceful and clear yourself. So even if no one else notices, you can have yourself a wonderful life.

# Day 4: Instinctive Improvement

Instinct is underrated in our culture. We favour careful planning and execution, and we seek to provide predictable outcomes so the thinking mind can see the future and feel safe. When instinct is used (or seems to be), it is often confused with rashly acting out an emotion, like following an urge. This is not true instinct and it gives instinctive action a bad name.

Today I hope to clarify what truly instinctive action means and to encourage you to experiment with a more instinctive life. But what is instinct anyway?

From a mindful point of view, instinct is action that is in alignment with the present moment. We could say that this action arises with the present moment, so the problem and the solution are not separate, they arise together.

When you look without thinking at a situation and the right action becomes obvious, instinct is at play.

In your workplace, the idea of being more instinctive or intuitive may be seen as a bit flaky, but today you will see how effective this way of approaching work (and life) can be.

There are a couple of prerequisites for instinctive action. First, you must be aware, alert and present, right here and now. You cannot respond effectively to what is happening now if you are busy thinking about something else after all!

Second, you must allow the present situation to be as it is. When you stop resisting what is, you can look at it with a deeper curiosity, out of which action may arise.

And finally, you need to allow the time and space for that action to present itself, which often means to wait and watch and listen.

Recently, in my own work, I was with someone who had experienced a situation they couldn't accept. This friend of mine was sad, angry and upset, and my mind wanted to fix it. But knowing that this would be the worst possible response, I stayed as present as I could, listened and waited.

As my friend spoke and as I listened, she started to slow down and appear calmer. She sat with the emotions arising and found some space of her own. And in the silence between us, some ideas started to arise. Thoughts flew into my mind and they seemed appropriate to the situation. As I shared those ideas with my friend, she was thankful and said that they were perfect. She adapted those ideas herself and applied them, and she said that this helped a great deal.

Speaking to another friend who was at a loss, I did the complete opposite. My mind said 'I know how to fix this' and I immediately stopped listening. I waited for her to pause, and then I jumped in, giving the answers. She changed the subject and never asked me about it again.

The difference between these two approaches is that in the first, I waited and trusted that an answer would come if it was needed. In the second, I pulled out an answer as soon as I could, relying on thinking (memory, past) and stepping out of true listening (awareness, now). The first approach allowed space for something new to flourish, the second probably made things worse. Which approach do you generally use?

## Activity – Playing the Game

Today, I want to introduce you to an easy way to play with this instinctive way of working in a way that is very low risk. After all, it might seem unsafe to become all instinctive rather than thinking things through, so let's start with a small experiment.

Just for one hour the next day you are at work, act as if you are playing a game, rather than working. Pretend that you want to win the game, as this will ensure that you do your best work, but make the tasks you do and the interactions you have a part of this imagined game.

To be successful in this game, you will need your wits about you. You will need to watch carefully, to listen carefully, and to pay attention to what is happening. You will need to be mindful as you play.

And as you work with that intense awareness, let yourself act in the way that seems best for the situation. Forget the rules of your mind, the way you have done things in the past, forget your fears, just for a moment. Instead, let the right action arise out of your awareness of the present situation and see what happens.

And when you have finished, take a moment to reflect. Was being instinctive *that* risky, was it *that* different? Or is it something you do at times, without really noticing?

In truth, we act on instinct more often than we notice, but because the mind keeps chattering as we act, it can seem as if the thinking, the logical decision-making, came before, not after. This week, I invite you to check in your own experience how often you act without thinking, and to see what happens when you act this way more often, and on purpose.

Make life into a game, and let your responses come directly from your experience this very instant.

## Day 5: Becoming Me

Work is a wonderful field for conflicts to arise. There are competing demands, people with different agendas and the competition that arises when mind-identified humans spend many hours in the same room!

There are two types of conflict, however: external conflict and internal. External conflict is what happens when you and somebody else don't agree on something and there is a disagreement. Internal conflict is what happens when the external conflict gets turned into a dramatic inner story, providing your mind with many hours of stress, anxiety and entertainment as the drama continues to unfold, long after you have gone home!

And this inner conflict, which is the only problematic type, occurs because of a simple fundamental error that can easily be remedied. In fact, inner conflict contains within it a simple reminder that can put you back on the right path, if you use it correctly.

And so today, we will explore the power of using conflict skilfully to bring your focus back to you, which is where you need to be.

First, though, let's understand how internal conflict arises, because the process is quite paradoxical. Inner conflict happens when your attention moves outside of yourself, which seems all mixed up, but it's true.

When your manager demands something unreasonable of

you, and your mind latches on to that, creating inner drama, your focus goes to your manager. You might picture her making those demands, you might plan your future response, or you might just mentally complain about what she did. All of these responses draw attention out of your experience right now and into the external world, in this case, your story about your manager.

And when your attention moves from you to the external world, it feels uncomfortable. Really, you are drifting into thinking, and so there is no one there in your experience to notice what is happening now.

Lost in that story, stress arises, and usually we blame that stress on the seeming cause – the other person. But the true cause is that we have checked out, we are not at home, and so there is a feeling of disconnection, which no one else can cause.

Other people can't make this happen. They can do all sorts of things, but they can't make you leave your inner experience, so it's totally your responsibility, which is wonderful news.

However, it isn't as if you can just decide to remain mindful in the midst of outer conflict and that will be that. Your mind will keep drawing you into creating inner conflict, so it is important that we find ways to work with this pattern and use it to our advantage.

In every conflict, there is a critical signal that can remind you to come back to you, and that signal is stress. When you feel uncomfortable internally, when you feel anxious, fearful or angry, this is a reminder that you have checked out, and that you have the power to check back in.

### Activity – Checking In

Take a mindful breath now and pay close attention to your body. Scan every part for a few breaths and notice what is happening in you right now. Feel your way from your toes to your head and back down again, and keep breathing as you do so.

Notice what tension is there in your body, and when you find a feeling of tension or stress, go into it with your attention. Don't try to change anything, just be with it. Each sensation has a purpose; it can bring you back to the present moment, so just come back and enjoy being present.

Leave any stories about what created that sensation alone, simply be there as the witness of it, experience it fully. Make your inner experience more important than any story about the outside world. In other words, return to you.

When you use the stress that arises when inner conflict comes up as a reminder to return to you, it can become a wonderful gift. Be alert for any negativity that may arise in you during your work day and, rather than indulging stories about that negativity, experience it.

When you use stress and conflict to bring you back to your own experience of life right now, you can take full responsibility for your own happiness. You can stop putting the power in the hands of others by focusing on what they 'need' to change, and embrace your own self instead.

When you do this, you restore and strengthen that connection with yourself and with life now. Outer conflict then loses its power to make you unhappy, and when you do feel negative, this becomes an opportunity to connect once more.

So there is no possibility of failure in this practice. If you feel negative, use that as fuel. If you feel positive, use that as fuel. And most important of all, keep bringing your attention back to your experience right now, no matter what is happening in the outside world.

## Day 6: The Momentary Journey

In some ways, the way I experience work is a paradox. I notice that change seems to happen over time, that I seem to be growing as a person, and at the same time, nothing changes. There seems to be movement in a certain direction, and yet, without my story of the past, there is only this, right now, nothing else exists.

This paradox may sound confusing or frustrating, but when you live it, it makes perfect sense. When you don't analyse and think about it, this seeming conundrum is quite straightforward.

And so I like the phrase 'the momentary journey', because my work life is a process that seems to continue over time, and that journey is always happening right this instant.

When you look at your own development at work, you may find this metaphor helpful, because it allows you to embrace two seemingly contradictory movements: the drive to improve and the acceptance of things as they are. Today we will explore how to reconcile these two ways of being so that you can continue to learn and grow, even after you make peace with life as it is now.

Take a breath now and smile. Look around you and notice, with interest and curiosity, all that surrounds you, all that has been provided for you. Notice yourself too. See how perfect you are, exactly as you are now? You are exactly the age you should be, the weight you should be and the height you should be. Your IQ and your income are just right, whatever your mind may say. Unless the universe made a mistake, you must be exactly correct right now.

Keep breathing and see: if you are not thinking about what is missing or what is wrong with you, if you are too busy breathing and smiling and enjoying yourself, then what happens to those so-called imperfections? They only exist in your mind. No thinking, no imperfections, right?

But, your mind may say, if you stop thinking about your imperfections, how will you ever get better? That's the wonderful thing about being on a momentary journey. There's always the next step.

Actually, it's always *this* step, but it's a step nonetheless. That step is a movement in a particular direction, but on this journey, we value each step equally. Normally, humans value the *last* step most highly, because it seems as if the destination is what matters. But if you have been around for a while, you will know that all destinations are only stopovers before the next journey begins. There's only one final destination and it's not usually something people look forward to!

We all have projects at work, as well as strengths and areas we could improve on. But when you stop thinking about your so-called shortcomings, you can approach those areas from a different place. You can be completely at peace with your current performance and also take delight in finding ways to improve.

## Activity – Improving Perfection

Close your eyes for a moment and make a mental list of all your so-called weaknesses at work. If you can't think of any, ask a colleague to help you out!

My list of imperfections (to give you an example), looks like this: I am sometimes disorganised, often a bit sloppy, regularly late and sometimes uncommunicative.

Take attention into your body and move from thinking to experiencing life right now. Notice all the sensations happening inside you, be present and aware. Smile.

Notice how those imperfections fade when you stop thinking about them? In fact, they're just stories.

Keep smiling and breathing, and as you do, picture one thing you could try to make a small improvement in each area. For me I could: check email first thing in the morning, talk more with my manager and email my team once a day.

This doesn't feel like a list of 'shoulds' because it arises from a place of allowing. Instead, it feels like a list of possibilities, of opportunities that I could play with, and this brings a sense of energy and excitement to the journey ahead.

This is the opposite of beating yourself up, but it's not like burying your head in the sand either. Instead, it is an embrace of the energy of contentment and enthusiasm, as if you were celebrating your wonderful self while gleefully looking at the next step of the journey, this step.

This approach, of course, is countercultural, as we have been told that improvement only comes from finding and remedying weaknesses. But in fact, starting with complete acceptance and celebration of you as you are now brings energy and excitement to the possibilities that might come next.

Love yourself, just as you are right now, and you will improve faster than you can believe.

## Day 7: Doing Peace

As we come to the end of our journey together, I want to close with perhaps the most baffling and powerful practice of all: the practice of doing peace. This is the art of taking action from a place of complete calm and serenity, regardless of the situation or the activity, an approach that is radically different to what we have been taught to do.

Thinking our way through activity is so ingrained in humans that it seems a little strange, perhaps, to do things peacefully, in the state the Zen masters called 'non-thinking'. We are used to thinking about what we do, and mentally resisting the things we don't like. This may take the form of complaining, thinking about something else or looking forward to the next thing, all of which are acts of resistance against the activity at hand now.

After all, if you are deeply and peacefully engaged in doing something, then what space can there be for complaining, or for wishing for something different? If life is just as you would wish, then these activities make no sense. It is only our dislike of the present moment that makes them seem reasonable.

So we can call this way of being 'thinking', and we all know what that is like. There is another state, which seems a little better, in which we zone out, drifting away somewhere else mentally as we wilfully ignore the activity we are doing.

This isn't mindfulness either, it is more like mind*less*ness. We are still thinking, but those thoughts are unrelated to what is happening now. Many people drive in this state, arriving with no memory of how they got to their destination.

This way of being may be less stressful, but it is rather dull. It is not rewarding or fulfilling because we are not engaged fully in our daily work.

The third way is to do peace, to act without thinking about what you are doing, but let's walk through this step by step. To act without thinking doesn't mean to be rash or disorganised in your work. You might still take some time to plan and consider the best way to approach a particular task or project.

But during the activity itself, there is no thinking going on. Thoughts may still occur, but they happen as a sort of background noise, like having the radio on as you drive, without absorbing all your attention. Your attention flows into the task at hand, and the doing itself becomes the most important thing.

Try the following activity and see how this way of doing compares with thinking or zoning out.

## Activity – Doing Peace

Pick an activity that you do on a regular basis at work. This could be attending a particular meeting, completing paperwork or something else. Choose something that you habitually run away from mentally, or complain about, or try to get through.

But today, act as if this task is the most important part of your day. Pretend that your whole mission in life is to do this activity with care and attention, as if everything depended on it.

Keep a lighthearted attitude, though, like caring for a child or a puppy – both important tasks that we still can enjoy.

As you do what needs to be done, shift attention away from thinking and into your senses. Look carefully and clearly. Listen with attention. Feel the movements of your body as you act. Don't think about it, just do it as well as you can.

And as you do so, notice what it feels like to do peace rather than thinking, take note of how this experience differs from your usual way of doing.

What was it like to drop thinking and act with such awareness and precision? I am sure that you might have drifted off a few times, but overall, how did that feel? Was anything lost in terms of quality or skill? And what was gained?

As I have practised this over many years, a couple of interesting things have happened to me. Firstly, there are no tasks that I 'hate' anymore, whereas there used to be many! I don't rush through so-called 'chores' in the search for something better and I feel more or less present in what I do, most of the time.

There is great peace in this way of doing; in fact, we could say that peace is taking action through you!

Just imagine never being in a rush (although you can still move quickly when needed). Imagine enjoying each task rather than mentally complaining or wishing for something else. And imagine a world in which this way of doing things is the norm, rather than the exception.

This world, in fact, is entirely possible, and it starts with the approach of you and of me, right now. So, now that you have experienced both ways of doing things, which will you choose, and how would you like to live your life from here on?

With the tools in your hands now, the choice is entirely yours.

# Conclusion

What a journey we have taken together over the course of this book! It has been as much a learning experience for me as for you, and I thank you for coming along for the ride.

At the heart of our journey was a critical assumption: that life, and therefore work, is there to bring us into a deeper state of mindfulness, or at least that we can approach it in this way.

Of course, work has other purposes, like providing money for food and shelter, and finding fulfilment through contributing to something larger than ourselves, and these purposes can continue alongside our mindfulness practice. But if you make mindfulness the core of your life, and let everything else be a bonus, then those extras will take care of themselves quite well.

In fact, becoming peaceful, alert and content as you work can't help but improve every aspect of what you do.

We have covered varied ground and used a range of activities on our journey, and it might seem as if there are many skills to learn. But actually, each activity is designed to bring you to the same place, awake and alert in the here and now. So don't feel as if you need to master or even attempt each one, just use the ones that resonate with you. The key is to keep practising, so use whatever feels right at the time, just keep bringing attention out of thinking and into what you are doing right now.

And finally, before I go, be gentle with yourself! These concepts are easy to understand, but our minds are complex and the old patterns are strong, so it may take some time to feel a sense of mindfulness seeping into your everyday life. It took me many years to experience this, but with these simple tools (and probably your superior intellect), you will progress much faster if you just keep practising.

So give yourself a hug from me. What you are doing is the most valuable thing any human can do. You are changing the entire world, and I thank you.